D0514509

DEFENDING
WALES

THE COAST AND
SEA LANES
IN WARTIME

ALAN PHILLIPS

AMBERLEY

First published 2010

Amberley Publishing Plc
Cirencester Road, Chalford,
Stroud, Gloucestershire, GL6 8PE

www.amberley-books.com

Copyright © Alan Phillips 2010

British Library Cataloguing in Publication Data.
A catalogue record for this book is available from the British Library.

ISBN 978 1 84868 845 2

Typeset in 10pt on 12pt Sabon.
Typesetting and Origination by FONTHILLDESIGN.
Printed in the UK.

W

DEFENDING
WALES

F 6 MAR 2012

Sp

Contents

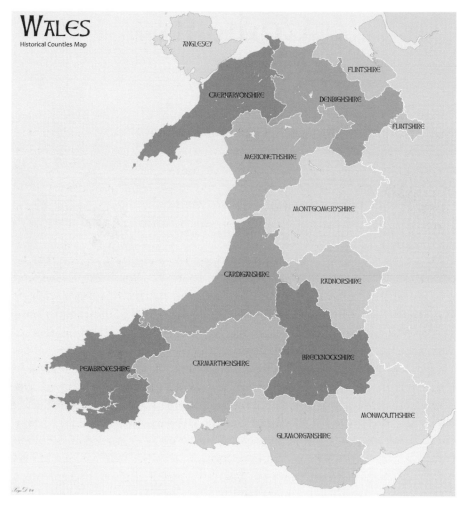

Map of Wales.

Introduction

Britain has always depended on its sea lanes for trade and security. Over the centuries, settlements were built around the coast which eventually developed into ports and harbours, taking full advantage of the ever growing sea trade. In Wales, ports expanded and became important for the export of coal and steel and the import of valuable commodities. These ports and industrial areas became major towns and centres of wealth for the nation.

This book covers the importance of the sea lanes around Wales and the approaches to the British Isles. Being in a westerly location, Wales had three important arteries around its coast: the Bristol Channel, with its important ports, St George's Channel, and the Irish Sea, with its route to Mersey Side and the north-west industrial area. These sea lanes were vital to commerce and had to be protected at all costs.

Up until the First World War, the threat of invasion was the main concern of the British, but during the war a new threat emerged: the enemy submarine, which caused havoc in the Atlantic and around the Welsh coast. In the Second World War the U-boat still remained a threat, but as Wales was now within range of German bombers based in occupied France, its towns, ports and industrial hubs also became targets. Welsh air defence began during the First World War, with airships and biplanes, and ended during the Second World War, with flying boats, four-engine patrol aircraft and fighters. This book briefly traces the air defences of the Welsh sea lanes against enemy submarines, and the defence of the ports and harbours against enemy bombers.

Several prominent locations in the country became sites for airfields; in wartime, numerous Allied squadrons operated day and night from these airfields in the battle to keep the sea lanes open for shipping and the skies clear of enemy bombers.

CHAPTER 1

Early Defences of the Sea Lanes

Being an island nation, the sea has always played an important role in the survival of the British people. From early times, the nation has depended on its sea routes for trading food and raw materials from abroad, and the transportation of large quantities of goods. The sea lanes around our coast became the motorways of yesteryear.

For well over three hundred years, British merchant shipping was attacked or confiscated by its enemies, whether Dutch, French or Spanish. It was even a target for privateers and pirates. Even in those early days, merchant shipping was advised to sail together where possible and have the British navy escort them in certain areas.

In times of war, a blockade was a favourite strategy to make sure the enemy stayed in its own ports, but as usual there were flaws; smaller vessels used to slip out undetected. During the eighteenth century, especially at the time of the Seven Years War, a total of nearly 3,000 merchant ships, ranging from the large ocean-going merchantmen to the smaller coastal cutters, were sunk or captured by the enemy, some even in sight of the shore.

The UK depends on its sea lanes being kept open at all times, not only from abroad but also around its coast for coastal shipping. For centuries the islands have been at the mercy of various invaders, from the Romans to the Normans and even the French during the Napoleonic Wars. Wales, just like the rest of the British Isles, was threatened by foreign invaders; its ships were constantly attacked as they sailed the coastal routes. It was not long before the early chieftains and princes erected wooden towers in prominent positions on the coastlines of their principalities. Eventually, the wooden towers were replaced by permanent stone watch towers manned by armed men.

The biggest construction of fortifications in Wales took place during the reign of Edward I. The castles were built not only to deter invaders from the sea, but also to control the frequent Welsh uprisings. The castles were

Harlech Castle is a good example of early coastal defence in Wales.

Caernarfon Castle is perhaps the best example of an early Welsh coastal fortification.

built between 1277 and 1307 and stretched from the English border in the north to the English border in the south. All the castles were built on or near the coast, or in a prominent position protecting an estuary. Usually armed sailing boats were stationed near the castle entrance to deter any attacks from the sea.

Sheltered inlets and deep estuaries had always been ideal shelter for ships in bad weather, but they were also ideal places for enemy shipping to hide from the British Navy in times of conflict.

In north Wales, the Menai Straits became an ideal shelter for shipping and the port of Holyhead became essential for links with Ireland. In south Wales, perhaps the most famous shelter was Milford Haven, which was used by shipping throughout the ages; its small inlets gave rise to settlements and harbours. The inlets became especially useful in Elizabethan times during the threat of the Spanish Armada; ships based at Milford pursued the Spanish ships escaping northwards up St George's Channel.

The first attempt to fortify a waterway came during the reign of Henry VIII, when basic brick forts known as blockhouses were constructed at the entrances to the ports and waterways. Up to the nineteenth century, coastal defences consisted of look-out towers, some of which were built of stone but most of a wooden construction. Ports were usually protected

Martello Tower in the Haven.

by blockhouses (gun emplacements) located at entrances to harbours, and armed with various calibre gun batteries.

As in most cases, coastal defences in Wales were not the absolute deterrent. In 1797, a small French Legion under the command of Colonel William Tate landed at Carreg Wasted near Fishguard in Pembrokeshire. The invasion force consisted of 600 regular troops and 800 convicts released from French prisons to fight for France. The original plan was to land near Bristol with instructions to burn the town and cause mayhem in the surrounding area. Due to poor navigation and bad weather, it was a failure from the start. An alternative plan to land troops in the Cardigan Bay area and march to Chester and Liverpool was considered. The four French ships anchored off Carreg Wastad Point with the intention of landing at Fishguard, but when they were fired on by a coastal battery they decided that the town was too heavily defended. Colonel Tate ordered his men to land at Carreg Wastad, a few miles away.

Several of the invading French were captured by local people, who were led by a local heroine, Jemmima Nicholas. The Pembroke Fencibles and the Cardiganshire Militia, led by Lord Cawdor, rounded up the rest of the invasion force over the next few days. This was the last attempted invasion of Britain.

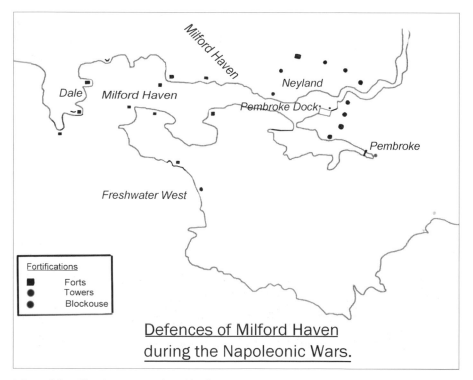

Map of fortifications around Milford Haven.

Napoleon's conquests in Europe and the increasing threat of invasion became a priority for the British military. Although the south coast of Britain was the nearest to continental Europe, the French landing at Fishguard in 1797 spread fears of an invasion throughout the rest of the country. As a result, coastal areas and inlets such as Milford Haven, the Severn Estuary, Holyhead, and the Menai Straits, became of great strategic importance. In 1815, the only Royal Dockyard in Wales was officially opened, with the first ships, HMS *Ariadne* and *Valorous*, launched on 10 February 1816. Both were twenty-eight gun sixth rate wooden sailing vessels.

Even after the defeat of the French and Spanish fleets at Trafalgar, there were still fears about the growing strength of certain foreign naval fleets and the chaos they could inflict on British shipping. It was not until the Napoleonic wars that the concept of true protection and defence became a reality.

Fortresses and gun emplacements were built around the country, mostly on the shores of southern England. The best examples in Wales are in the Milford Haven area, protecting the natural port of Milford and Pembroke. This was not only a working port but a base for the Royal Navy warships. On either side of the estuary, several forts and gun emplacements were built, supplemented by gun towers in strategic positions.

Thorn Island Fort.

West Blockhouse, Milford Haven.

After the Napoleonic wars and years of general unrest in Europe, the country witnessed perhaps the largest construction of forts, gun towers (Martello), and gun emplacements in any century. These became known as Palmerston fortifications or 'Palmerston Follies'.

Due to continuous unrest on the continent, especially in France, another war seemed inevitable. The government realised that most of the nation's Royal Dockyards were vulnerable to attack from the sea. The new dockyard and ship building yards at Paterchurch, which later became known as Pembroke Dock, located on the Milford Haven inlet, was one such yard. The fortifications became a priority and were built mainly on the south coast between 1850 and 1870 at considerable cost. However, most of these fortifications were never called upon to fire a gun in anger. In Wales, Pembrokeshire, especially Milford Haven, was given the strongest defences with such forts as Dale, Popton Point, and Hubberston. The Milford forts consisted of 220 guns of various calibers, positioned to allow overlapping fire.

In north Wales the most famous coastal fortification is Fort Benlan. It is located north of Dinas Dinlle overlooking Caernarfon Bay to protect the southern entrance to the Menai straits. Other heavily defended sites

Gun emplacement on a Martello Tower.

Fort Belan with its own harbour on the entrance to the Menai Straits. (*Fort Belan*)

included the area around Tenby, the Gower Peninsular, Swansea, and Port Talbot: all important sea ports.

Despite the prodigious budget spent on coastal defences, the best and most effective instrument for defending coastlines and protecting trade routes was the warship. Small, fast, armed sloops and the larger frigates were stationed in prominent positions around the coastline, especially near ports and inlets of significant importance.

Throughout the centuries, merchant shipping was a prime target in times of war and peace. Piracy was another cause of concern in peacetime. Buccaneers and adventurers became wealthy in war by plundering enemy shipping with the approval of the state, but in peacetime their methods and brutality was deemed unlawful and they were hunted down by the authorities.

Another group of individuals that caused great concern to the nation was smugglers; they operated in a number of locations around the coast of Wales. Perhaps the most deadly of all groups were the 'wreckers', who tricked unexpecting vessels by lighting false beacons to lure ships on to rocks so their cargo could be looted.

In Wales, the Severn Estuary was perhaps the most important seaway, with the ports of Cardiff, Barry, Llanelli, Swansea and Chepstow, and Bristol on the English side. Further west there were the ports of Tenby.

St Catherine's Fort, Tenby.

Aerial photo of Tenby showing the wall, town, castle and St Catherines Fort. (*via Tenby Council*)

Gun emplacements and barracks were constructed on Flat Holm and Steep Holm Islands in the estuary. Together with artillery batteries on Lavernock Point, south of Cardiff, and Brean Down Fort in Somerset, they had complete control of shipping in the estuary.

Haverfordwest and Pembroke, as well as the port of Milford Haven, with its natural shelter, became major naval ports. Whenever there was a threat to shipping, naval ships sailed immediately to their defence, but usually arrived hours after the event.

In the twentieth century, the concept of defending the coastline and shipping changed. Admittedly, placing gun emplacements in strategic positions along the coast continued, but new weapons had been added to the defence armoury: aircraft, radio and, in 1940, radar. But shipping, vital for the nation, was still at risk.

In the eighteenth and nineteenth centuries the main enemy of merchant shipping was other surface sailing boats. Warships were the main defence, but, as time went by, airships, aeroplanes and flying boats were able to protect the sea lanes. The First World War, however, introduced a new menace, the dreaded U-Boat, which sunk millions of tons of valuable commodities with a great loss of life.

It was inevitable that Wales would once again play its part in defending the sea lanes around the western side of Britain. In both World Wars, sites were chosen to build airfields and landing areas for airships and

Old and new defence: an airship flying over Caernarfon Castle. (*Gwynedd Archives*)

aeroplanes to defend the coastline and the shipping lanes of St George's Channel, the Severn Estuary, the Bristol Channel, the Irish Sea, and the Western Approaches.

Even in the twenty-first century, the sea lanes are still important for trade, and shipping is the best method of transporting large volumes of cargo.

CHAPTER 2

The First World War

At the beginning of the twentieth century, Britain's economy depended on overseas trade. The interception of commercial shipping was regarded as fair game in time of conflict to any nation possessing ships. For the defence of the nation and its commerce, the Royal Navy possessed the largest and most modern fleet in the world, consisting of battleships, battle cruisers, cruisers, destroyers, submarines and all sorts of auxiliary vessels. At the time, the senior service was considered capable of protecting all the vital sea routes for commercial shipping.

In 1914, Europe erupted into a World War the likes of which no one had ever seen before. It would eventually involve every British family, every hamlet, every village and town in one way or the other. Thousands upon thousands of young men eagerly joined up, answering Kitchener's call, 'Your Country Needs You'. Most of them were never to see their home or country again. With the young able bodied men away at war, the women became the workers of Britain in all sorts of factories, especially in those dealing with munitions.

In August 1914, there was an unprecedented level of activity throughout Wales as the country prepared for war. Local Yeomanry were mustered almost immediately and put on standby. Army camps sprung up in every available site ready to cope with the large influx of eager volunteers ready for training. Coastal defences from the Gower Peninsular to Pembrokeshire and from Gwynedd to Flint were beefed up and manned. Old forts dating back to the Napoleonic wars were reactivated and manned. By the end of the year, tented army camps had sprung up in almost every county, just like newly erected villages.

In the early part of the war, the greatest threat to the British coast and shipping were warships of the German High Seas Fleet. The enemy began its shipping attacks in the traditional way by using its surface raiders, mostly cruisers, where the Allied naval forces were weakest. However, within months the German cruisers and raiders were hunted down and

The convoy system was developed during the First World War.

A German U-boat of the First World War. (*IWM*)

sunk by the Royal Navy. Others were blockaded in their home ports with the rest of the German High Seas Fleet.

A new threat emerged to shipping: the German U-boat. It was capable of slipping out of the German bases undetected, and harassing British shipping around the coast and beyond.

The First World War U-boat campaign began on 4 February 1915, when the German High Command announced that merchant shipping in the vicinity of Britain and Ireland was a legitimate target. Up to then only warships of Britain and France had been targeted by enemy submarines and surface ships. However, due to American pressure (they were neutral at the time), concessions were made so that hospital ships and all ships flying flags of a neutral country were exempted.

During the war, enemy submarines took a heavy toll on Allied shipping in every theatre. To begin with, a gentlemanly principle of evacuating civilians before sinking the ship was adopted, but it soon developed into torpedoing cargo ships without warning.

The shipping lanes around the Welsh coast were of the utmost importance to the British war effort. Through these channels passed the essential imports of food and raw materials for industry. Coal, shipped from southern and northern coal fields on coastal freighters, was vital for industry, and Welsh coal was the main power source for the Royal Navy ships based around the UK, before their conversion to oil fuel.

RMS *Leinster* was sunk by U-123 on 10 October 1918. (*via Anglesey Maritime Museum*)

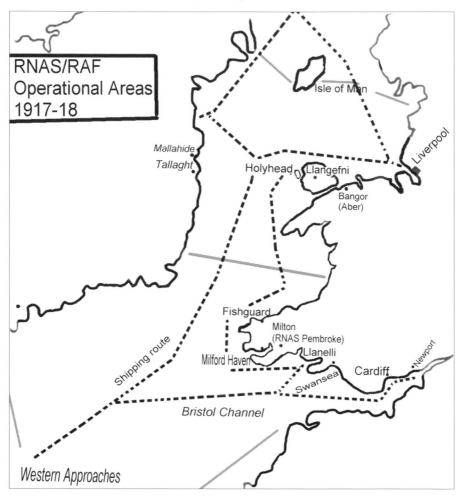

RNAS/RAF
Operational Areas
1917-18

Isle of Man

Liverpool

Mallahide
Tallaght

Holyhead Llangefni

Bangor
(Aber)

Fishguard

Milton
(RNAS Pembroke)

Llanelli

Milford Haven

Cardiff

Newport

Swansea

Shipping route

Bristol Channel

Western Approaches

Map of the operational patrol areas around the coast of Wales.

The Bristol Channel and Western Approaches was a high risk area as it was on the major sea routes to the important south Wales and West Country ports. In the north, the Irish Sea, St George's Channel and Liverpool Bay were tied to Belfast, Holyhead, Liverpool and the industrial areas of Merseyside. These ports, and the Welsh and West Country ports, were given the highest protection in both World Wars.

The German U-boat was not truly defeated, but the Allies were able to keep the menace under control and provide a sort of protection for the ships. After the convoy system was reactivated with naval escort and air patrols in 1917, the numbers of sinkings dropped; in eighteen months, 1,300 merchant ships were sunk in the Atlantic and in home waters. Three quarters of the merchant shipping lost in 1917–18 were sunk fifty miles

A Zero type airship escorting a convoy.

off the coast of Britain and France. Four out of every ten were just ten miles off the coast, usually in sight of land.

In the early years of the First World War, the Admiralty believed that only warships were capable of protecting the sea lanes from German surface raiders and U-boats. At that time, the aeroplane was in its infancy and not regarded as a potential contender in fighting U-boats, but there was soon a massive improvement in aircraft design and reliability. A warship would often take considerable time to reach a stricken ship or a periscope sighting, whereas an aircraft could be on site within a short time. This was the logical thinking which changed the Admiralty's view of the aeroplane, and inspired it to place the development of maritime aircraft at the forefront of Naval strategy.

Neither the warship nor the aeroplane nor the airship completely defeated the U-boat, but they were a significant deterrent and many ships were spared.

CHAPTER 3

Airships

The German submarine campaign against merchant shipping in the First World War began on 4 February 1915, when the German High Command announced that *any* shipping in the vicinity of Britain and Ireland was now open to attack. All the shipping lanes around the coast of the British Isles became prime targets for the U-boats and surface vessels, and, as several sea lanes were in the vicinity of the Welsh coastline, the nation played an important part in protecting the convoys.

Liverpool was one of the main ports in the British Isles that drew a considerable interest from the enemy; within weeks of the announcement three ships were sunk off Liverpool and further two more were sunk off the north Wales coast. In south Wales, coastal ships conveying coal from the ports of Barry, Cardiff, Llanelli and Swansea became legitimate targets. Several were sunk either by U-boats, or mines laid by them. During this period, several ships sailing in the Irish Sea reported sighting submarine periscopes, and even a German surface vessel was reported.

The most formidable deterrent against submarines was warships armed with depth charges, but their response time was not ideal. Several hours could pass between a submarine sighting and a warship's arrival on the scene, and by then the ship under attack had usually sunk and the submarine was on its way home. The only solution to the menace was the aeroplane. However, in 1915, there were no planes available with sufficient endurance, capability or reliability, so the airship filled the gap.

For some years, the Admiralty had been using various dirigibles for fleet patrols operated from ships and shore bases, and found they had remarkable endurance provided the weather was fine. After numerous experiments and modifications at Farnborough, several airships were armed and adapted for sea patrols. Eventually, the Sea Scout type went into limited production.

To accommodate the airships, the Admiralty built a number of air stations throughout the British Isles. Two were built in Wales: one in Anglesey, in

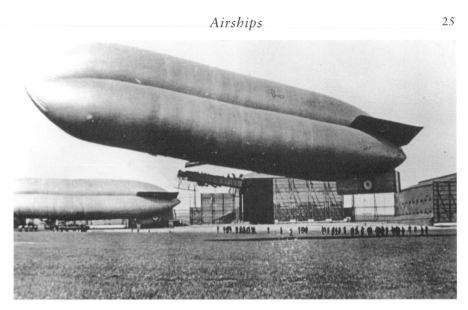

Two Coastal Class airships at RNAS Pembroke. (*FAA Museum*)

the north, with a subsidiary station at Malahide outside Dublin, and one in Pembrokeshire, in the south, with a subsidiary at Killeugh, Co. Cork in Ireland. In Pembrokeshire, the Admiralty acquired 228 acres of land near the village of Milton and Sageston, just off the main road between Pembroke and Carmarthen, as a site for an airship base, RNAS Pembroke. Several sites in Anglesey were considered; eventually some 200 plus acres of farmland were acquired three miles from the town of Llangefni. For four years the air station was called RNAS Bodfordd and Gwalchmai, Llangefni, but RNAS Anglesey was eventually adopted, which not only confused the enemy but everyone else.

Llangefni airship station (RNAS Anglesey) was commissioned on 26 September 1915 as part of No. 14 Group, responsible for the protection of the British coastline. The station consisted of an airship shed of 120 x 318 feet, complete with windshields on both ends and associated workshops. Gas production units and wooden accommodation huts were also constructed. A Bessoneau hangar was added later to accommodate the DH-4 and DH-6 aircraft. The Llangefni patrol sector covered an area from Bardsey Island to Dublin and up as far as the Isle of Man and Morecambe Bay. The station's first commanding officer was Major George Scott, who eventually became Deputy Director of Airship Development, but tragically lost his life in the R-101 crash in France in 1930.

Airships were urgently required in the area as, in 1915, six merchantmen were sunk in the north Wales area. The largest of these was SS *Hartdale*, a 3,839 ton cargo ship bound for Alexandria in Egypt, torpedoed by U-27, 7 miles south-east of South Rock.

Sea Scout Zero SSZ-50 at Llangefni.

T. B. Williams and the crew of Sea Scout SS-31.

The first airship to base at Llangefni was Sea Scout No. 18, crewed by Flight Sub-Lieutenants W. Urquart and Kilburn, flown in from Kingsnorth on 26 September. However, SS-18 was seriously damaged on 9 October 1916, when it struck a cow while landing in an adjoining field. It then struck a control car, and drifted out to sea with the crew unable to do anything. Eventually the airship came down off Ireland on 22 October; unfortunately one rating was drowned.

The next airship to arrive at Llangefni was SS-22, with a BE2c car, on 5 November 1915, captained by Flight Sub-Lieutenant E. F. Turner. SS-22's claim to fame was that it achieved diving from 1,100 to 100 feet in

Sea Scout SS-24 landing at RNAS Anglesey, Llangefni.

56 seconds, an exceptional performance for an airship of the day. SS-22 left Llangefni for Wormwood Scrubs in April 1917, and was eventually handed over to the Italian Navy on 2 June 1917.

Also in 1915, SS-24 with a BE2c car arrived at RNAS Anglesey, captained by Sub-Lieutenant Scroggs. The airship remained at Llangefni flying patrols and convoy protection until 11 July 1917, when it departed for Luce Bay for patrol work in the north Channel. It was eventually decommissioned in July 1918.

SS-25 was another airship to land at Llangefni in 1915, captained by Sub-Lieutenant T. B. Williams. Returning from a long patrol on 23 November 1917, it made a forced landing and was badly damaged. SS-25 flew a total of 149 hours between August and December 1917, and 77 hours in 1918 before the Armistice.

Within weeks, the full complement of four Sea Scout airships had arrived at the station. Having established themselves at Llangefni, they began escorting the Liverpool bound convoys and the Dublin to Holyhead ferry.

RNAS Anglesey received its last Sea Scout on 4 November 1916, SS-33 with a Maurice Farman car built at Vickers, Barrow, in January 1916. The airship came from Luce Bay to relieve the over-worked Llangefni crews. However, during a convoy patrol in April 1917, it was forced to land at Cemlyn Bay due to engine failure, sustaining slight damage.

For the latter part of 1916, RNAS Anglesey airships were involved with escort duties and long patrols. During this lull the station was involved in

Deflation accidents were common. In this photograph, SS-25 is being towed to Holyhead by the launch *Amethyst*. (*PRO*)

SSZ-37 being manhandled at RNAS Pembroke. (*B. Turpin*)

experiments with hydrophones: underwater microphones lowered from the airship into the sea, which could detect the sound of a submerged vessel. Although hydrophones were never used during the First World War, the technology has proved invaluable since.

In Pembrokeshire, the base at Milton did not take shape until January/February 1916. It was very similar in construction to Llangefni, with two 120 x 318 feet corrugated iron hangars, together with large windshields. Two lots of hydrogen storage tanks were constructed adjacent to the hangars. Wooden huts and canvas workshops were constructed, as well as a number of tented accommodations for the personnel. In April 1916, RNAS Pembroke was classed as fully operational.

During the early months of 1916, the base became mostly a stopping point for airships attached to various warships patrolling the Irish Sea. This arrangement was quite useful to Milton personnel, as it gave them considerable training in handling the crafts.

The first airship to arrive at Pembroke was SS-15 with a BE2c car (cupola) on 25 April 1916. The airship was built at Wormwood Scrubs in August 1915. SS-15 operated out of Pembroke on shipping patrol and U-boat searches in the Bristol Channel and well into the Western Approaches. On one such patrol, on 18 January 1917, it ran into bad weather and was wrecked off Lundy Isles.

Another SS-42 arrived at Pembroke for trials on 28 August 1916. However, while landing after a long patrol on 15 September 1916, the airship broke away from its moorings with the pilot, Flight Lieutenant E. F. Monk, aboard. The airship flew for 100 miles and rose at one point to

Sea Scout SS-15 in a hangar at Milton (RNAS Pembroke). (*B. Turpin*)

the height of 8,000 feet; by now the pilot was hanging to the undercarriage for dear life. It eventually crashed at Ivybridge, Devon.

The Sea Scout airships had been hurriedly developed by the Admiralty to counter the U-boat threat to shipping. It was realised that the SS were just a stopgap with limited capabilities. A larger airship was required with greater range and endurance, with twin engines for reliability and capable of carrying more armament. The Coastal class was developed by using two Avro 510-seaplane fuselages joined together. The four-manned cockpit car was powered by two 150 hp Sunbeam engines on either end, one a tractor, the other a pusher. The first trial flight took place on 26 May 1915, from Kingsnorth. In the course of the next few months, several modifications were made, including upgrading the Sunbeam engines. Fully loaded, the Coastal's could carry half a ton of bombs or depth charges for 12 hours. Maximum speed was 46 mph, with an endurance of nearly twenty hours. The airship was armed with two Lewis .303-inch machine guns.

It was soon realised that the Coastal types would be more beneficial based at Pembroke, as its patrol area extended into the Western Approaches. The first Coastal to be based at Pembroke was C-6, which arrived by rail from Kingsnorth on 29 May 1916. The airship arrived in crates at Haverfordwest rail station and was transported by road to RNAS Pembroke. Within a week, the airship was operational; it convoyed

A coastal airship on convoy patrol. (*IWM*)

Coastal Class CC-6 taking off from RNAS Pembroke. (*B. Turpin*)

patrols and anti-submarine sweeps in the Irish Sea and the Western
Approaches. The sight of the coastal airships to the weary convoys turning
the southern coast of Ireland was very reassuring, as no ship was ever
sunk or attacked when airships were about. The second Coastal class (C-
3) arrived at RNAS Pembroke on 9 June. One of the first actions involving
a C type was in November 1916, when C-6 dropped two small bombs on
a possible periscope sighting east of Cork. On 2 December 1916, during
another long patrol in poor weather, C-6 had to make a forced landing at
Germag, near Mullion. After slight repairs it returned to Pembroke. C-6's
last patrol was on 23 March 1917; at the end of a long, 11 hour patrol, it
developed engine trouble and crashed into the sea with no survivors.

The last of the Coastal Types (C-5A) arrived at RNAS Pembroke for
trials on 27 August 1917, having been reassembled after an incident at
Longside in January when the carriage was totally destroyed. It remained
at Pembroke until 24 March 1918, by which time it had accumulated over
605 hours on patrols and convoy duties.

During 1917, enemy submarine activity around Wales had increased
considerably. In February alone, six coastal vessels were sunk near Bardsey
Island, causing some concern in the Admiralty and putting extra pressure
on RNAS Anglesey to combat the threat.

In June 1917, most of the SS series were replaced by the Mark 2, known
as Sea Scout Pusher airships. They had an increased gas volume, over
70,000 cubic feet, and had a crew of three. Only six of the type were built;
three of which replaced the older type at Llangefni (SSP-1, 5 and 6).

Coastal C3 at RNAS Pembroke

A Milton based C-3 non-rigid airship.

The first to be based at Anglesey was SSP-5 on 18 January 1917 from Wormwood Scrubs. Previously, the airship, together with SSP-2, was modified to take a black envelope (85,000 cubic feet), and fitted with a silenced engine for secret night flights in France. SSP-6 arrived at RNAS Anglesey on 16 June 1917 from Wormwood Scrubs, with the charismatic T. B. Williams piloting the craft. During its stay at Llangefni, the airship logged 320 hours. While on a patrol on 16 March 1918, SSP-6 developed an engine failure and crash landed in the Irish Sea. Fortunately, the crew was picked up by a passing ship, and the airship was taken in tow. Being lighter, it was just like running with a kite; the airship took to the air cutting the towrope and floated south-eastwards. It flew over mid-Wales and eventually landed in a wood in Chichester, Sussex. The envelope was deflated and returned to Llangefni. On 12 April 1918, SSP-6 was to partake in training at the Airship Training Centre at RNAS Cranwell, but was forced to land near Blackburn due to another engine failure, and was badly damaged. The last SSP to arrive at Llangefni was SSP-1 on 5 July 1917 from Kingsnorth. It was one of the fastest airships in the RNAS inventory with a speed of 52 mph.

For long patrols, a mooring station was built at Malahide, near Dublin, and at Killeaugh, Co. Cork, which allowed the airships not only an opportunity to refuel and rearm, but also gave the crew a short, but invaluable rest bite.

In 1917, twenty-seven ships were sunk by German U-boats in the RNAS Anglesey/Pembroke patrol area. Mines laid by U-boats claimed several

A Sea Scout Zero non-rigid.

ships along the Welsh coast right up to the end of the war, some even after the Armistice. The cargo vessel SS *Lucia* struck a mine laid by UC-65, off St David's Head on 11 February 1917.

The Admiralty was constantly searching for the ultimate patrolling airship, and, after various classes, developed the Submarine Scout Zero type. This was the reason for the limited production of the successful SSP class. The SS Zero was a non-rigid airship with a total volume of 70,000 cubic feet. The beam was 30 feet, and the overall height was 44 feet 6 inches. The length of carriage was over 18 feet. Total fuel capacity was 102 gallons, which gave it an endurance of 16 hours at 50 mph, or 40 hours at 20 mph. It had a crew of three in a modified B.E. 20 fuselage.

Towards the middle of 1917, the SS Zero class was issued to most air stations, but there was still a shortage of airships. As a result, SS 42 was rebuilt at Wormwood Scrubs and returned to Pembroke in August 1917 as SS-42A, to supplement the other airship based at the station. Unfortunately, SS-42A was yet again involved in an incident on 12 September, when it crashed into some farmyard buildings during a night landing. The crew, Flight Sub-Lieutenant Cripps and his wireless operator, were unable to abandon the craft; it drifted out to sea in the direction of Carmarthen Bay and was wrecked near Bull Point. Both crew members lost their lives.

SSZ-17 was the first of the class to be based at RNAS Pembroke. It was transported by road and assembled at the station on 7 August 1917.

A Sea Scout Zero type, Anglesey based SSZ-35.

After the initial trials and familiarisation, it was flying convoy and anti-submarine patrols. Between August and December, the airship flew 448 hours, and another 53 hours in three days in January 1918. However, Z-17 was destroyed in a shed fire on 3 January. Part of the airship sheds were also destroyed, but these were soon repaired. SSZ-16 was another airship transported to Milton and assembled; it was first flown at the station on 19 August 1917. The airship flew a total of 1,403 hours from August 1917 to November 1918. Most of the patrols were monotonous without any sightings; boredom often crept in and, on a number of occasions, caused crews to take risks. One of these occasions was on 7 December 1917, when they sighted and attacked a surfaced U-boat which had fired on the airship. Instead of retreating to safety, the airship dived on the submarine with its Lewis gun firing. Fearing being bombed, the U-boat dived for cover.

In 1917, U-boat losses around the coast of north Wales were very few: three were sunk in the north Channel between southern Scotland and Ireland, especially in the Isle of Man area, and four in St George's Channel.

Two Zero types, SSZ-50 and 51, arrived at Llangefni on 13 March 1918, both from Kingsnorth. SSZ-50, while involved with a night landing exercise at Malahide on 1 April, had its envelope ripped. The airship was repaired and returned to Llangefni within weeks. More Zero class airships were despatched to RNAS Pembroke in the first part of 1918. SSZ-53 arrived on 21 March 1918 and flew a total of 917 hours; the last flight was in December 1918. The next Zero type to be based at Llangefni was SSZ-34, which arrived on 23 March 1918 from Howden. It remained at

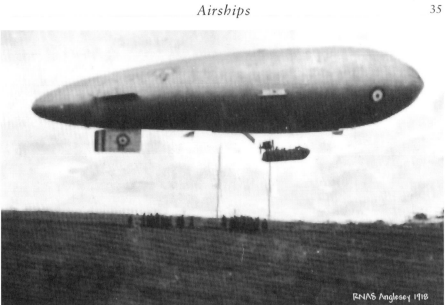

A Sea Scout Zero airship landing at RNAS Anglesey.

SSZ-17 about to take off from Milton. (*Fleet Air Arm Museum*)

Another RNAS Anglesey based airship, SSZ-51.

Anglesey until being deflated and struck off charge on 26 November 1918, by which time it had flown 859 hours on convoy duties.

With the formation of the Royal Air Force on 1 April 1918, all land-based air operations were handed over; as expected, RNAS Llangefni and Pembroke were transferred and became the responsibility of the RAF. Initially there were no changes whatsoever; the bases were still run by naval personnel and the airships still kept their original markings.

On 2 April 1918, SS Zero Z37 was despatched to RNAS Pembroke from Wormwood Scrubs. On 18 April 1918, SSZ-56 arrived from Howden, but returned to Howden in November. Llangefni's first SS Zero patrol took place on 18 April 1918, by Z-35, under the command of Captain Williams. After some 7 hours patrolling Liverpool Bay, it suffered an engine failure and the crew had no choice but to make an emergency landing. Fortunately, the airship came down near a fishing boat which eventually towed it to safety so it could be beached at Llandudno, where it was temporarily repaired and flown out to Llangefni for extensive repairs.

The first contact with a U-boat was made on 18 May 1918, when SSZ-50, operating out of RNAS Anglesey at Llangefni, located some oil slick in the sea near the Skerries off the coast of Anglesey. The airship dived to 300 feet dropping two 100 lb and one 230 lb bombs. The contact was reported to other airships in the area who relayed the message to patrolling warships. The destroyer D01 was first on the scene, dropping a depth charge pattern in the reported area, but no possible sinking could be verified. The search was continued early the following day by three airships from Llangefni. Some twelve miles off Bardsey Island, SSZ-51 located the wake of a periscope and sighted the dark shape of a submarine below the surface. As the airship reported the sighting to other crafts, it dived, dropping its bombs on the target. SSZ-35 also joined in the attack, but no hits were observed. Three American and one British destroyer arrived on the scene, dropping their depth charges in a wide pattern. Soon, debris and a large amount of oil rushed to the surface. After the war, records showed that U-boat UB-119 with its crew of 34 seamen perished under the Irish Sea on that particular date.

To cope with the large volume of work, RNAS Pembroke received another Zero craft (SSZ-67) on 22 May 1918, which flew to Milton from Kingsnorth.

On 27 May 1918, an enemy submarine was sighted some five miles off Pontllyfni, Gwynedd. Three Llangefni-based airships and two Royal Navy destroyers were despatched to the area in Caernarfon Bay to make a search. Airship SSZ-34 dropped a 230 lb bomb on some sea disturbance in the vicinity, followed by SSZ-51, working in conjunction with a destroyer, which dropped depth charges on suspicious bubbles on the surface. A submarine presence in the area was unlikely as sea disturbances were often caused by a submerge wreck or currents. After the war, no records could be traced of enemy submarines working in that particular area.

On 28/29 June, one of the longest endurance patrol flights ever recorded by any flying device was made by SSZ-35, with Captain Williams as pilot,

An air to air photo of the fuselage and crew of SSZ-67.

and Flight Lieutenant Farina and Air Mechanic Rawlins as his crew. The
26 hour 15 minute patrol flight took them to Northern Ireland, across
to Scotland, south to the Isle of Man, and across to Blackpool, where
they were observed from the promenade. The final leg of the flight was to
Liverpool and back to Llangefni, following the north Wales coast. As they
crossed the Anglesey coast, Lieutenant Farina decided to drop a bomb
on rock protruding out of the sea. Unfortunately the airship was flying
too low and a splinter from the exploding bomb punctured the envelope.
Fortunately, Captain Williams managed to nurse the airship back to base.
The majority of the patrols occurred in the Liverpool Bay area, escorting
troopships into Liverpool and Manchester.

Perhaps the largest cargo vessel to be sunk off the Welsh coast was SS
Ethelina, 13,257 tons, bringing iron ore from Spain to Barrow in Furness.
The vessel was sunk by U-103, some fifteen miles north-west of the
Skerries. In all, between January and November 1918, eighteen ships were
sunk around the coast.

In many circles it was felt that the age of the airship had come to an
end with the introduction of twin-engine aircraft such as the Blackburn
Kangaroo, Handley Page HP0/100, the Vickers Vimy and the twin-engine
Felixstowe F2A flying boat, which had reasonable endurance and could
reach an area faster than the airship. But there was still support from
certain quarters determined to prove the viability of such craft.

Breaking the endurance record was one way of increasing support for
the airship and, on 29 June 1918, SSZ-35 achieved this. It flew north from
Anglesey, across Scotland, down towards the Isle of Man, then eastward
towards Blackpool and Liverpool, returning via the north Wales coast to
Holyhead across Caernarfon Bay, down Cardigan Bay and the west coast
of Wales, finally returning to Llangefni twenty-four hours later.

During a patrol on 11 August, SSZ-37 from Milton made a forced
landing near Mumbles; the crew of three was rescued uninjured. The airship
was picked up by a Swansea-based Royal Navy patrol boat, and returned
to Milton for repairs. On 18 November 1918, SSZ-37 was involved in
towing trials with the naval vessel PL.61 in the Bristol Channel, to examine
the possibility of increasing the airship's range and endurance. SSZ-37
continued to look for mines after the Armistice, until it was deflated on 29
January 1919. The total flying time was 675 hours 30 minutes.

After initial crew training, SSZ-51 took part in convoy patrol in
Liverpool Bay and the Irish Sea. During one such flight on 2 April, the
propeller tore the envelope while the airship was landing, a common
problem with the Zeros. Three days later, the airship was forced to make
an emergency landing at Iselo because of a ripped envelope. On its final
patrol from Plangent on 15 September 1918, the envelope deflated, causing

SSZ-37 exercising with a warship in the Bristol Channel.

it to ditch in the sea, but the crew were rescued by an American warship, USS *Downs*.

Further attacks on U-boat sightings followed. On 27 May, SSZ-34 dropped a 230 lb bomb on a suspicious target, but a hit was not confirmed. SSZ-51 dropped bombs on some bubbles appearing in the water, again with no confirmation. After a long patrol on 28 July 1918, SSZ-67 landed heavily at Pembroke causing the envelope to be torn by the propeller. The airship was repaired and was later involved in covering American troopship convoys. The airship's last flight took place in December, after flying a total of 639 hours. Llangefni-based SSZ-50 was damaged yet again in a gale at the base on 4 October and, while on a patrol on 18 November, it was forced to land at Aberaeron.

On 10 October the final sinking in the Irish Sea took place when the City of Dublin Steam Packet Co. morning mail boat, RMS *Leinster*, was sunk off the Kish Bank by the German submarine UB-123. The Kingstown (Dun Laoghaire) to Holyhead ferry was struck by two torpedoes, which sank her in twenty minutes with the loss of 501 passengers and crew, out of a total of 771. Most of the passengers were military personnel returning to duty from leave. This was the greatest loss of life to occur in Welsh waters. That particular day, bad weather with gusty winds prevented any airships from taking off from Llangefni, which might have deterred UB-123 from attacking the *Leinster*.

SSZ-35, another of Llangefni-based airships, was lost at sea on 17 October 1918, owing to a torn envelope some fifteen miles north-west of Holyhead. SSZ-42 was based at Mullion, but after a forced landing

Shadow of a SS Zero airship flying over Milton village in 1919. (*E. Perkins via D. Brock*)

at Ilford Cammo near Christchurch on 17 June 1918, it required a new envelope and modifications. It was despatched to RNAS Pembroke in November 1918 as SSZ-42A.

Another Zero type to be based at Pembroke was SSZ-46. It was initially meant to go to Folkestone, but was sent to Milton to cover the American troopships coming from the States. During one patrol it was fired on by an escorting warship, having been mistakenly reported as a Zeppelin. The airship flew a total of 648 hours, the last flight taking place in November 1918.

There is no record of any airship ever sinking a submarine, although several from Llangefni on Anglesey and Milton in Pembrokeshire were involved in various sightings and assisting surface ships to the scene. However, the airships' presence during escorting duties and patrolling was more of a deterrent than an actual threat. Most of the sinkings occurred when ships sailed singly, with no escort. Perhaps the airship's greatest enemy was the weather, together with serviceability which caused most of the accidents and fatalities. The airships based in Wales were, rather fortunately, well outside the range of German seaplanes, which were shooting down several crafts on the south and south-east coasts of Britain.

With the war coming to an end, and land-based aircraft becoming more advanced and capable of longer distances, it was felt by some that the airship era was coming to an end. So there was an all out effort to prove that the dirigible was still an effective weapon. On 21 October 1918, all U-boats were recalled to their bases, ending a gruelling submarine campaign around the coast of Wales.

When the Armistice came on 11 November, there was great joy at both the Llangefni and Pembroke bases, although the airships continued to patrol for the rest of the year and for most of 1919, especially on mine patrols.

On 21 November 1918, SSZ-53 was patrolling an area in the Bristol Channel between the Gower Peninsular and Ilfracombe, when it spotted three mines floating on the surface. The airship Lewis machine gun was unable to explode the mines, therefore the location was sent to the mine sweeper based at Swansea. However, by the time the sweeper arrived, two of the mines had collided and exploded, leaving the third to be dealt with by the Royal Navy.

Thousands of German and Allied mines had been laid around the coast of the United Kingdom. Most had broken their anchorage and drifted into the sea lanes. A trawler operating out of Milford Haven was struck by a floating mine in January 1919. Once an airship located a mine the crew would fire at it with two .303-inch Lewis machine guns to explode it. In one week, Milton Zero airships destroyed at least twenty-three mines in St George's Channel and Carmarthen Bay. Part of the celebrations was the flight of an airship under the Menai Suspension Bridge.

A close-up of a Sea Scout Zero fuselage.

After the war both bases remained opened until October 1919, when all the airships were deleted from operational use.

The following airships were stationed at RNAS Anglesey (Llangefni) and RNAS Pembroke (Milton):

RNAS Anglesey:
Sea Scout   SS-18, SS-22, SS-24, SS-25.
Sea Scout Pusher   SSP-1, SSP-6, SSP-5.
Sea Scout Zero   SSZ-31, SSZ-33, SSZ-34, SSZ-35, SSZ-50, SSZ-51,
                       SSZ-72, SSZ-73.

RNAS Pembroke:
Sea Scout   SS-15, SS-37, S-42.
Coastal Type   C-3, C-6, C-5A.
Sea Scout Zero   SSZ-16, SSZ-17, SSZ-28, SSZ-36, SSZ-37, SSZ-42A,
                       SSZ-46, SSZ-52, SSZ-53, SSZ-56, SSZ-67, SSZ-76.

Coastal Class CC-4 non-rigid airship, based at Pembroke.

CHAPTER 4

Seaplanes

Fishguard harbour became a Royal Naval Air Service seaplane base to combat the mounting enemy submarine attacks on Allied shipping in the Irish Sea during 1917.

Since 1916, attacks on coastal shipping by enemy U-boats had trebled. By the time a warship reached the scene, the U-boat had disappeared, either to the open Atlantic or to the safety of the rugged coastline of neutral southern Ireland, which they often used as shelter. The only solution was to set up seaplane bases at strategic positions along the British coast.

Several areas in Wales were considered. Among these were the Menai Straits and the beaches at Rhyl in north Wales, Milford Haven and Burry Inlet in the south, but only Fishguard Harbour, with its sheltered bay, was finally chosen. Fishguard Harbour was already a thriving port serving Cork and Waterford in southern Ireland.

RNAS Fishguard was officially established on 1 March 1917 by Squadron Commander John T. Cull DSO, RN, of the Admiralty Air Department Special Service. Initially, RNAS Fishguard came under the control of Commander in Chief Plymouth. On 3 April 1917, the RNAS seaplane western wing came under the authority of Wing Commander E. L. Gerrard's headquarters at Devonport, overseeing the bases at Cattewater, Port Melon, Newlyn and Fishguard, as well as the airship stations at Mullion and Pembroke. In November 1917, Fishguard and Pembroke became the South-West Group, under the command of the Senior Naval Officer based at Milford Haven.

The Admiralty's intention was to base two Royal Naval Air Service flights at Fishguard consisting of six seaplanes, three Sopwith Baby or Fairey Hamble Babies and three Short Type 184 Seaplanes, but as the war progressed and the submarine threat became more intense, the number was doubled. All belonged to Nos 426 and 427 Coastal Patrol Flights of No. 245 Squadron, with Major F. Denham Till as commanding officer.

Map of Fishguard Seaplanes Patrol Area.

Map of Fishguard-based Seaplanes' patrol area.

The seaplane station at Fishguard. (*National Archive*)

A replica of a Sopwith Baby seaplane.

The main types of seaplanes operated from Fishguard by RNAS and the RAF were Sopwith Babies, Fairey Hamble Babies and the Short 184s. The Sopwith Baby was the smallest of the seaplanes. It had a single seat and was powered by a 110 hp Clerget engine, which gave the aircraft the speed of 92 mph and an endurance of two hours in reasonable weather. It was armed with a single .303-inch Lewis machine gun and up to 130 lbs of bombs. The Fairey Hamble Baby was a development of the Sopwith aircraft, with the ailerons being replaced by a trailing edge flap enabling the aircraft to take off and land at lower speeds, therefore reducing a strain on the engine. It was powered by the same Clerget engine giving similar speed and endurance to the original design. The Short Type 184 was the largest of the Fishguard seaplanes. The two seat aircraft was powered by a 220–240 hp Sunbeam Mohawk or Maori, or Renault engines, which gave it a top speed of 88mph and an endurance of nearly five hours. Its armament consisted of a .303-inch Lewis machine gun mounted on a Scarfe or Whitehead mounting in the rear cockpit. The seaplane was designed to carry a 14 inch torpedo under the fuselage, or up to 260 lbs of bombs.

The seaplane base consisted of one small hangar, constructed of a wooden frame covered with canvas, and was used mostly for aircraft maintenance rather than storage, as the seaplanes were usually moored in the bay. All accommodation was also under canvas, except the officers were messed in the nearby Bay Hotel.

A Short 184 on slipway.

The first aircraft to arrive at Fishguard was a Blackburn built Sopwith Baby (N1011) seaplane on 30 March 1917. Within days, it began flying patrols in the vicinity, mostly escorting ferries from Cork in southern Ireland. The second Sopwith Baby (Blackburn built N1033) arrived on 16 April 1917. Unfortunately, this aircraft, piloted by Flight Lieutenant R. E. Bush, crashed seven days later, before it flew one sortie. Lieutenant Bush took off from the bay as normal, but soon a power failure developed and he was unable to gain sufficient height to clear power lines from a powerhouse supplying the base. The aircraft swerved to avoid a building and struck a cliff face, bursting into flames. Private B. Blackburn of the King's Regiment based at Fishguard was on sentry duty and managed to pull Lieutenant Bush from the burning aircraft, but tragically Flight Lieutenant Bush died from his injuries on 23 April. Although the flight was recorded in station records as a test flying a new engine, the aircraft carried two 16 lb bombs, which fortunately did not explode. It seemed that several tell-tale submarine signs had been seen around the coast near the Fishguard to Rosslare ferry route, and all aircraft were armed and put on a constant state of readiness.

Both types of seaplane were rather delicate machines; the slightest rough seas or gusty winds were enough to cause damage or flying accidents. On 24 April 1917, Short 184 (9086) was damaged while taxiing in rough weather, causing the aircraft nose to dive into the sea; fortunately there were no casualties. Another Type 184 (N1149), piloted by Flight Sub-Lieutenant R. G. Clarke, crashed in bad weather into Windy Hill near Fishguard.

One of the first recorded attacks on a U-boat was on 23 November 1917, when Flight Sub-Lieutenant H. F. Delarue, piloting a Fairey Hamble

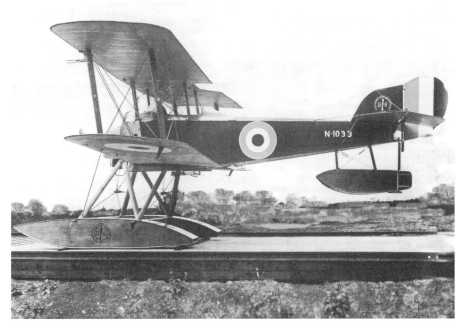

A Blackburn-built Sopwith Baby.

A Short 184 seaplane taking off in rough seas.

Baby (N-1199), was patrolling some 12 miles north-west of Strumble Head and spotted a periscope wake heading in the direction of the Irish ferry. From a height of 1,000 feet the pilot dived on to the spot at full throttle, shutting off his engine at 500 feet and releasing his two 65 lb bombs. The engine was restarted and the seaplane returned to observe the result of the attack. One bomb failed to explode but the second exploded within about 10 feet of the disturbance. White bubbles and a large area of disturbed sediment appeared on the water, but there was no sign of what seemed to be a periscope wake. Three other armed seaplanes were despatched from the base to the area but nothing was sighted.

Also in November 1917, two aircraft from Fishguard went to the aid of a trawler, which had been attacked by a surfaced U-boat. By the time the aircraft got to the scene, the submarine had gone and the trawler was limping back to port. On their return to Fishguard, however, one of the aircraft spotted what looked like a periscope trail in the sea. The Short 184 made a low pass and dropped two 25 lb bombs; at least one of the bombs exploded but they could not confirm a kill.

On 8 December 1917, another submarine contact was made by Flight Sub- Lieutenant W. G. Westcott and K. F. Alford in a Short 184. Two bombs were dropped on the wake but it was not possible to confirm a kill.

During the First World War, radio communication between aircraft and base was in its infancy. Carrier pigeons played a vital role in the communication between seaplanes and the shore base. The single-seat

Homing pigeons were used as communication between aircraft and base. (*Tommy Bennett*)

aircraft would land on the sea, providing it was calm, and release the pigeon with the message attached to its leg. While in the two seat type, the pigeon would be released by the observer while the machine was in flight. At Fishguard, two airmen were responsible for looking after the pigeons.

Patrolling over water in the flimsy seaplanes of the First World War was extremely risky; the dangers of technical reliability, weather and pilot disorientation caused most of the accidents. One such accident happened on 21 February 1918, when Flight Sub-Lieutenant Cyril Gordon Duckworth, flying a Fairey Hamble Baby N1457, failed to return from a patrol in Cardigan Bay. The aircraft was last sighted between Cardigan Head and New Quay, which was outside the safe patrol radius for a Hamble Baby. It seemed that Duckworth had run out of fuel and landed his seaplane in the sea. When the St Dogmaels lifeboat reached the reported position there was no sign of the wreckage or the pilot. The majority of the aircraft was eventually salvaged and the rest was washed up on shore later, but Sub-Lieutenant Duckworth's body was never recovered.

According to records, the seaplanes based at Fishguard made several sightings, but there is no record of any submarine being either damaged or sunk. However, their presence was a deterrent as, on a few occasions, surfaced submarines made a hasty retreat when a seaplane appeared on the horizon.

Another U-boat sighting occurred on 22 March 1918, when Sopwith Baby N1127 and Short 184 N1638, patrolling an area north-west of

A Sopwith Baby being lifted out of the water at Fishguard. (*FAAM*)

Fishguard, spotted the usual periscope wake in the sea. At once, the Sopwith manoeuvred into an attack position and dropped a single 65 lb bomb; a heavier 100l b bomb was dropped by the Short 184. Neither of the pilots could confirm a kill, but the submarine was probably damaged. Short 184 N2765 was on what was classed as emergency patrol in the same area when the pilot observed a large disturbance and air bubbles coming to the surface of the water. The aircraft dived on the contact dropping one 100 lb bomb, but again, no confirmation of a kill could be attained, although the disturbance ceased.

On 13 March 1918, Air Mechanic F. G. Hayward was flying as an observer in a Short 184 and spotted a surfaced U-boat north of Fishguard. As the aircraft dived on the submarine, it was greeted by light machine gun fire from the U-boat, but no damage was inflicted on either the submarine or the seaplane. Air Mechanic Hayward was again in action on 20 April, when Short 184 N2765, piloted by Lieutenant E. S. Smith, dropped two 100 lb bombs on a submerged submarine positioned north-west of Dinas Head.

Prior to August 1917, operational statistics for patrols flown by seaplanes from Fishguard were included in South-West Group's statistics. After this date, statistics were kept for the seaplane station itself. A typical example of operational statistics for March 1918 is as follows:

Week ending 2nd March – A total of five patrols were flown, one was a routine search, two were emergency patrol and two had to be aborted just after take off because of cloud cover. Duration of the patrols was 3 hours and 28 minutes covering about 240 miles.

Week ending 9th March, eleven patrols were flown totalling 10 hours 21 minutes and covering a total of 681 miles.

Week ending 16th March the weather improved considerably enabling thirteen patrols to be made covering a distance of 1,418 miles and lasting over 21 hours.

Week ending 23rd March – The weather remained good therefore nineteen patrols were flown during the week covering 2,199 miles and lasting 33 hours.

Week ending 30th March a total of eleven patrols to Bishops, Smalls, St Brides, Cardigan Bay and to Bardsey Island were made covering a distance of 1,473 miles and lasting 21 hours 58 minutes.

These were exceptionally good statistics for one month for the station compared with the record for January 1918, when the unit only flew ten sorties covering only 839 miles, lasting 12 hours due to bad weather.

With the forming of the Royal Air Force on 1 April 1918, RNAS and RFC came under one independent authority. All RNAS assets and personnel

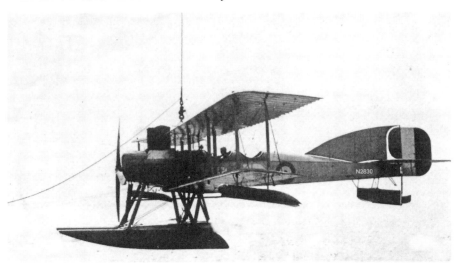

A Short Type 184 being hoisted ashore at Fishguard.

were transferred to the new organisation. The station at Fishguard became part of the No. 14 Coastal Operation Group and the unit was reformed into Nos 426 and 427 Flights under No. 77 Wing RAF on 20 May 1918. On 30 August, the two flights were merged to become No. 245 Squadron Royal Air Force.

By April 1918, the squadron had standardised on the Short 184 seaplane, which was regarded as more suitable to long range patrols and capable of carrying a crew of two, which was essential for such missions. During the first week in May, another submarine was reported in the Cardigan Bay area and was attacked by a Short 184, again with inconclusive results.

Short 184 N2765 notched up considerably more flying hours than most of the seaplanes based at Fishguard, but on 10 May, after a lengthy patrol, it smashed its tail float in a forced landing in fog.

On 29 June, a large patch of oil was spotted on the surface by an airship returning from a patrol. Short 184 N2908, piloted by Lieutenant Carr, was vectored to the position and dropped one 100 lb and one 280 lb bomb on the slick, but again, the attack was inconclusive.

Positive results were very rare, but on 6 July the squadron had a success when Short Type 184 N2830, crewed by Lieutenant E. A. Eames and Air Mechanic Hayward, spotted a sea disturbance in a north-western direction. The aircraft dived, dropping a 230 lb bomb on the position; within a minute, oil and air bubbles were observed rising to the surface, indicating that the submarine had been damaged. After the war, a U-boat was recorded as being damaged in the vicinity and had to make for port for repairs. Throughout the rest of the month and in August, there were five further incidents of aircraft dropping bombs on oil patches and periscope wakes.

What is believed to be the last recorded action involving Fishguard seaplanes took place on 3 September 1918, when Short Type 184 N2908 observed some oil slick and air bubbles in the sea off St David's Head. The seaplane dived, dropping two bombs on the suspected position; the aircraft remained in the area for ten minutes but saw nothing else, and eventually returned to base.

On 16 September 1918, SS *Serula*, a 1,388 ton cargo vessel, sent out an SOS that it had been struck by a torpedo. Two Short 184 seaplanes were despatched from Fishguard to the scene, but were unable to make any contact with a U-boat. However, they were able to direct a trawler and life boat to the scene to pick up survivors.

Most of the anti-submarine patrols undertaken by aircraft of No. 245 Squadron from Fishguard involved hours of monotonous searching for tell-tale signs such as oil slicks, surface sea disturbances, a periscope and its wake or even a surfaced submarine, which was a bonus. According to the station log, between 15 June and 9 November 1918, No. 245 Squadron flew a total of 865 patrols lasting approximately 1,703 hours, and covered some 39,522 miles, covering an area from Milford Haven to the Llyn Peninsular. The busiest week was the week ending 6 July 1918, when the Short 184 seaplanes flew twenty-four anti-submarine patrols lasting over 88 hours, and covering a distance of 5,171 miles, mostly in the Cardigan Bay area. It was not until after the Armistice that the general

After the formation of the RAF on 1 April 1918, the Short 184 became the standard equipment.

public knew of the splendid work done by the personnel based in camps such as Fishguard.

It was reported in May 1918 by the HQ at Milford that, from reports gathered by aircraft from Fishguard and Milton and the airships patrolling the seas, as well as ships of the Naval anti-submarine flotillas, they knew of the whereabouts of twenty-three enemy submarines in their controlled area. Most of the report was geared to uplift the population's morale by spreading the news that the U-boat menace had been overcome. The actual figures for U-boat sinkings were far below these statistics.

When the war ended in 1918, the base at Fishguard was dismantled and its personnel and equipment were transferred, leaving no evidence whatsoever that a seaplane base had ever existed. However, according to local residents, a few of the concrete moorings did exist for some time afterwards, and were used by local fishermen to moor their boats. They too disappeared with the subsequent redevelopment and strengthening of the sea defences. At the time of writing, only the concrete slipway remains.

Aircraft based at Fishguard between March 1917 and October 1918:

Blackburn built Sopwith Baby and Fairey Hamble built Baby.
N1011, N1033, N1124, N1433.
N1199, N1205, N1457.

Short Type 184 Seaplane.
N1086, N1149, N1683, N1684, N1742, N1797, N2657, N2658, N2659, N2790, N2796, N2828, N2830, N2842, N2843, N2907, N2908, N2940, N2941, N2942, N9032, N9033, N9086.

There were usually not more than seven aircraft stationed at Fishguard at any one time, as they were often distributed between other seaplane bases.

CHAPTER 5

Land-Based Aircraft

As the First World War progressed, Allied shipping losses continued to rise at an alarming rate. The airship patrols and ships of the anti-submarine flotillas provided reasonable cover in the channels and approaches to the United Kingdom, but there was a blind area nearer the coast. U-boats of the era had limited time submerged and therefore had to surface to re-charge the batteries for the submarine electrical motors and enable the crew to breath fresh air on a regular basis. During this period the submarine was very vulnerable to attack from the air. Also, what was known as inshore area became one of the favourite killing grounds for the U-boats as coastal shipping tended to sail close to the shore without any air or sea escort whatsoever.

In 1915, the Admiralty was faced with the ever-growing problem of enemy submarine activity around the British coastline. Several ships had been attacked and sunk, so pressure was put on the Admiralty to combat the submarine threat and keep the sea lanes safe. Therefore, all out efforts were put in action to develop land bases for airships and land-based aircraft. However, priority was given to the airship bases, which were thought to be more suitable for the task.

It was not until 1917 that the U-boat threat to coastal shipping was realised in full. Admiralty maps plotting U-boat activities and sinkings showed, since the introduction of the convoy system and airship patrols, the enemy had changed its tactics and the majority of merchant ship losses were within ten miles of land. The heaviest losses were on the north-east coast, the south-west, and around the coast of Wales.

During December 1917, enemy submarines off the coast of Anglesey sank nine vessels of various tonnages. The situation was no better around the south Wales coastline; colliers leaving the coal ports of Barry, Llanelli and Cardiff became prime targets for the German U-boats.

Aircraft of the period had a very limited range, payload and reliability, and were not suitable for long range patrols. They were, however, ideal

The Sopwith 1½ Strutter served with RNAS at Pembroke.

for inshore patrols. As the result of an Admiralty inquiry and pressure from the government, a series of seaplane stations and airstrips were built in prominent locations in the United Kingdom to supplement the existing airship stations. The bases were manned by Royal Naval Air Service personnel, and equipped with aircraft withdrawn from the front line squadrons. At the time, the RNAS's modern equipment was limited as all new aircraft entering service were required on the Western Front. However, in 1917, the Airco DH-4 and the Sopwith 1½ Strutters had been replaced and withdrawn for secondary duties in the United Kingdom.

It was reasoned that if coastal shipping lanes were patrolled regularly by aircraft at about twenty minute intervals, it would be enough to deter U-boats from attacking. First choices of aircraft were the Sopwith 1½ Strutter or the Airco DH-4 bomber, thought highly of on the Western Front. Initially, few of the type were issued to these Special Duties Flights, but the aircraft eventually allocated was the Airco DH-6, which had been withdrawn from the front line for training. Even in its training role, it had been superseded by the Avro 504. The RNAS had at least 300 DH-6s on their books which had become surplus to their training requirements.

On 29 April 1917, the first aircraft to arrive at Milton were six Sopwith 9700s, or, as it was better known, the Sopwith 1½ Strutter. These were naval bombers fitted with the RNAS Equal Distance Bomb Sight, which was regarded as the most sophisticated and most modern of all bomb

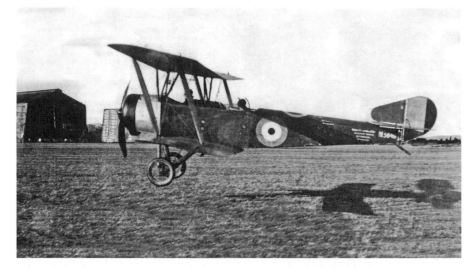

The Sopwith 1½ Strutter was a sophisticated fighter bomber for its time.

aiming equipment at the time. These Sopwith fighter-bombers got their name from an unusual arrangement of short and long pairs of centre section struts. The aircraft was powered by a single 110 hp Clerget engine which gave it a speed of 108 mph. It was armed with one Vickers machine gun and a Lewis machine gun, as well as four 25 lb bombs.

Initially, seven aircraft were destined for RNAS Pembroke, but, during transit, one aircraft was severely damaged when it made an emergency landing en-route to RNAS Pembroke.

The Sopwith Strutters patrolled an area between shore line and up to over 100 miles off shore, whilst airships patrolled areas beyond the aircraft's range and endurance. The patrol area covered by the Pembroke-based flight was the entrance to Milford Haven, the south coast of Pembrokeshire, Carmarthen Bay and the Gower Peninsula. North of the county, including the sea lane between Ireland and Goodwick, was covered by the seaplanes based at Fishguard. As with the seaplanes, most of the patrols involved hours of monotonous flights over the sea, searching for enemy submarines or occasionally escorting coastal shipping from the ports of Llanelli and Swansea around the Pembrokeshire headland.

The first Strutter patrol flight took place on 25 April 1917, with Squadron Leader Allaway at the controls. The flight lasted 1 hour, 10 minutes, covering an area from St Govan's Head to Pendine Sands. On 12 July 1917, two Strutters were on patrol in an area some seventy-five miles south of Caldey Island, when one of the aircraft spotted what seemed to be a periscope wake on the sea surface. At once the aircraft dived, dropping two 100 lb bombs on the surface disturbance. Both aircraft circled the spot

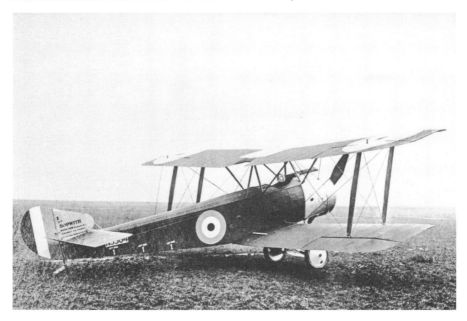

Sopwith 1½ Strutter.

and an oil slick was observed on the surface. The second aircraft instantly dropped two 100 lb bombs on the slick, observing two large explosions. Unable to stay as their fuel was running low, they returned to Milton. Later that day, an airship returning from a patrol over the area could not see any debris or oil slick. On 4 August 1917, the flight suffered its first casualty when Squadron Leader Allaway failed to return from a patrol in Carmarthen Bay.

The Admiralty came to the conclusion that both airships and land-based aircraft could work together, operating from the same base as they did at Milton. This arrangement was also intended for RNAS Anglesey, but after some trials and surveying the terrain, it was found that the ground was too rough and needed extensive levelling, which would be too costly.

On 7 November 1917, six Airco DH-4 fighter bombers from Castle Bromwich in the Midlands were sent to join the airships at Llangefni and provide inshore patrols. However, things did not go according to plan. Due to bad weather, only two aircraft reached north Wales; one landed on Traeth Lavan near the village of Aber, while the other, piloted by Second Lieutenant Bernard Carter DSO, crashed within sight of the base. Unfortunately, the pilot was killed and his observer, Corporal Harold Smith, was badly injured. The other aircraft completely lost its way and decided to return to base in the Midlands. Great effort was made by the crew and local farmers to retrieve the stricken aircraft bogged down in

A Sopwith Strutter, taken from a Milton-based airship. (*Tommy Bennett*)

the wet sand on Traeth Lavan, but they were beaten by the incoming tide. After a few days, the engine was salvaged and the fuselage was set on fire.

Long patrols often affected the pilot's navigation. In November 1917, when a Sopwith Strutter (believed to be A-5277) was escorting two trawlers back to Milford Heaven, the pilot reported spotting an object on the horizon and went to investigate. The Strutter never returned to Milton and was believed to have crashed into the sea.

It was not until 1918 that a suitable landing strip for the land-based aircraft was found and built in north Wales. The landing site was situated in a coastal area between Bangor and the village of Abergwyngregin on the edge of the Snowdonia range. Fifty acres of land, consisting of most of Glan y Mor Isaf Farm, was requisitioned in May 1918.

Most of the airfields during the First World War were very basic and easy to construct. At Glan y Mor Isaf Farm, hedges were removed to provide an enlarged area for landing and taking off, and Bessoneau hangars were constructed, usually on the grass. These hangars were the most common types at the time as they were easily built; they consisted of just a wooden frame covered with canvas. Officers and other ranks were housed in various sized tents for accommodation. Stores, fuel and ammunition were stored in a site protected by sandbags and covered by a tarpaulin in nearby woods, away from the main site. Some farm buildings were requisitioned for use as a wireless room and for briefing of crews.

Liberty engine powered Airco DH-6, which served with No. 244 Squadron at Bangor (Aber) and No. 255 Squadron at Pembroke.

Milton, on the other hand, was more developed, with wooden huts, administration blocks, sick quarters, and a technical section already in operation with the airship station. Only three Bessoneau hangars and additional accommodation huts were built.

After the formation of the Royal Air Force on 1 April 1918, the Special Duties Flights / Coastal Patrol Flights were rearranged into six wings and an HQ wing. The first to be reformed was No. 68 Wing, 18 (Marine Operational) Group at Seaton Carew on the river Tees in June 1918. On 8 August 1918, Wales came under 77 Wing, 14 (Marine Operational) Group, with its headquarters at Haverfordwest, and the Special Duties Flight HQ at nearby Milford Haven. RNAS Pembroke kept its two flights, Nos 519 (A Flight) and 520 (B Flight) of No. 255 Squadron. There were two Seaplane Flights 426 and 427 of No. 245 Squadron at Fishguard Bay. Nos 521 and 523 Special Duties Flights were transferred from Llangefni to Aber (Bangor) to become Nos 521, 522 and 530 Flights of No. 255 Squadron. A minor move was made just before hostilities ceased on 18 October 1918, when five DH-6 moved to Tallaght in Ireland.

Aircraft allocated for the Special Duties Flights was Airco DH-6, perhaps not the best choice for the task. Between 15 August and 23 November 1918, in No. 244 Squadron three flights received twenty-four Airco DH-6 aircraft, six to replace those that had crashed. Also in August 1918, RNAS Pembroke received ten Airco DH-6 from naval reserve stocks to supplement the Strutters already on charge. A further three reserve aircraft

Airco DH-6 (RAF 1A engine).

were added to the squadron inventory before the Armistice. These bombers were much slower than the Sopwiths, but had a longer range and were more adaptable to patrol work.

Throughout August, Aber-based squadron was regularly patrolling the coastal sea lane extending from Anglesey to Liverpool Bay, usually taking over the patrol from the airships. On one such patrol, a ship reported a strange sea swell some five miles off the Great Orme, thought at the time to be a submarine submerging. Two DH-6s were sent to investigate and observed what was interpreted as a periscope wake. One of the aircraft dropped two bombs on the disturbance, but there was no sign of a U-boat.

The Coastal Patrol Flights operated under great pressure and difficulty. The flights were constantly over-worked, flying frequently one hour patrols. The units were never up to strength in either aircrew or mechanics, most of whom were unfit for active service in France. As there was a shortage of armourers, bomb loading was usually done by mechanics and general personnel, which resulted in bombs not being primed and the machine guns jamming more frequently than usual. Flight Nos 519 and 520 at Pembroke often used the armourers from the airship station.

On 23 August 1918, a DH-4 (F3350) crashed into the sea during a combined patrol with an airship from Llangefni. Luckily for the crew, the airship was able give direction to a rescue vessel from Menai Strait.

On 7 September 1918, No. 244 Squadron suffered its first fatal accident at the base when a DH-6 crashed just after taking off. The pilot, Captain Tuck, and his observer, Air Mechanic W. Shaw, were badly injured and taken to Bangor hospital where Shaw died from his injuries. The squadron lost another aircraft on 11 October, when C2074 crashed in Caernarfon Bay, killing both crew members.

As there is no surviving airfields log, it is very difficult to obtain much information about the base. It would appear that the squadron was involved in several coastal patrols and on a number of occasions went to the assistance of merchantmen in the area, but there are no records of any of the aircraft involved with enemy submarines. However, it seems that one patrol went to the assistance of an airship from Llangefni which had mechanical problems and was in difficulty.

The squadron's greatest difficulty at Glan y Mor Isaf Farm was serviceability. There was a shortage of trained mechanics and spare parts; from a peak in October 1918, the squadron had seventeen aircraft serviceable, but the numbers dropped within weeks to twelve, and, at one stage, to only two. Fortunately, by December, as the spares gradually became available, the figure was up again to a reasonable level, but by now there was a shortage of pilots as some had left to join other squadrons. Usually, the unit had twice as many aircraft as pilots to fly them.

The airfield itself caused a great many problems, especially during the winter months. As a result of a wet winter, with heavy rain and strong winds, flooding occurred regularly which made the base uncomfortable for its personnel accommodated in tents. For most of the time during the winter months, the airstrip was water-logged and unserviceable; on a number of occasions, aircraft became bogged down in the mud. At one point, the base was declared non-operational, which caused a stir in the Admiralty.

Serviceability at RNAS Pembroke was rather better, as at any time the squadron could provide at least 75 per cent aircraft for patrol. However, after Armistice on 11 November 1918, the importance of Special Duties Flights declined. For the next five weeks the flights were involved in mine searching along the coasts of Wales. Several mines, both British and German, had broken away from their moorings in rough seas and were drifting dangerously in the coastal sea lanes.

In November 1918, Airco DH-6 aircraft on charge to Nos 244 and 255 Squadrons were as follows:

No. 255 Squadron Nos 519/520 Flights.
B2781, B2786, B2789, C2067, C2076, C9415, C9523, F3351, F3353, F3357.

No. 244 Squadron Nos 521/522 Flights.
B2791, B2976, B2979, B3020, B3023, B3025, C6560, C6655, C6656, C7861, C7862, C7864.

No. 530 Flight.
C6560, C7796, C7800, C7861, C7863.

A month after the Armistice was signed, arrangements had been made for all anti-submarine flights and squadrons to be disbanded. The first to go were all the squadrons under No. 18 Group, with others following soon after.

In Wales, the two squadrons of No. 14 Group were also disbanded. These were No. 255 at Pembroke on 14 January 1919, and No. 244 Squadron at Bangor on 22 February 1919. During the next few months, the canvas hangars and tented accommodation were removed. The personnel, the stores, and all the equipment were removed by road to the railway station at Bangor. In May 1919, the land was released for farming and became Glan y Mor Isaf Farm once more.

The tactics adopted by the Coastal Patrol Flights/Special Duties Flights were highly successful. During 1918, there were 4,869 sorties flown on escort duties by RAF aircraft and seaplanes from various bases around the United Kingdom. Only two vessels were actually attacked by submarines during the period. Bad weather was perhaps the biggest problem; it prevented any flying, and the U-boat took advantage of the situation.

CHAPTER 6

The Second World War

Aircraft flying from airfields and bases in Wales and the West Country made a major contribution to the defeat of the German U-boat menace that preyed on merchant shipping in the Atlantic, Western Approaches and around the west coast. Although, in both wars, the Royal and Merchant Navies took the brunt of the battle against enemy surface warships, aircraft and U-boats, the Royal Naval Air Service in the First World War and the Royal Air Force Coastal Command in the Second World War played an important role in defending the sea lanes around the west coast of Britain from enemy submarines. By the end of the Second World War, with the advancement in radar development and air weaponry, aircraft had become the U-boat's greatest threat.

Wales, with its prominent westerly position, was an ideal location for airfields, and during the Second World War, Pembrokeshire, on the south-west coast, was often referred to as the world's largest aircraft carrier.

When the British Prime Minister, Mr Neville Chamberlain, announced in a radio broadcast to the world at 11.15 a.m. on 3 September 1939 that Britain was at war with Germany, most people in Wales were attending chapel or on their way back from a service. To many, the news came second hand, but by the end of the day nearly everyone in the land knew that war had been declared. It was great shock as a large portion of the population still thought there was hope for a peaceful settlement.

The majority of Welsh airfields were constructed from 1940 onwards, and for the next few years thousands of acres were acquired for the purpose. Every farmer dreaded the official notice declaring that part of his land had been requisitioned for the building of an airfield or army bases and training areas. Most of the land taken up was good, fertile farming land, but a great deal was only suitable for grazing. There were some reports of farmers offering such land for military use as they regarded it as unusable.

A brick-built pill box.

A stone-covered pill box at Dinas Dinlle, Caernarfon.

Army camps and training grounds sprung up in various parts of the country, which caused a great deal of inconvenience to people and communities. In some areas crime doubled, which kept the police constabulary busy.

Perhaps the saddest part of the requisition order was the number of families ordered to vacate their cottages and homes to make room for the airfields. In September 1941, two sisters were given forty-eight hours to vacate their home to make way for Withybush airfield. The cottage had been their family home for generations, but they were told blankly that all must sacrifice something in time of war.

Around the Welsh coast, the old watch towers of previous centuries were replaced by concrete and brick pill boxes, either housing machine guns or used for observation and manned by the British Army and Local Defence Volunteers (Home Guard). The Home Guard was established on 14 May 1940, and was comprised of enthusiastic veterans of the First World War and men of reserved occupation. Until their disbandment, they continued to patrol cliff tops and every inlet for signs of enemy activity. In other words, they became the ground coastal patrol.

Another volunteer unit that contributed to observing the enemy was the Royal Observer Corps, formed in 1939 to report any aerial activity, whether friend or foe. Observation posts were located usually ten miles apart, with a number around the coast.

As the war progressed, a string of Home Chain radar installations were built around Wales for the detection of shipping and aircraft. Various

Pill boxes became common structures throughout Wales.

The Observer Corps provided valuable service from 1940 onwards.

A searchlight block at Mumbles on the Gower Peninsular.

masts and aerials appeared on the skyline. Also, look-out stations became common around the coast, as did searchlight batteries and barrage balloon units near to towns and military bases. Invasion was still the main concern for the government, and a number of stop lines were built in Wales, although the largest concentration was in England, around the Home Counties. In Wales, there were nine constructed in 1940 as part of the Western Counties stop line system, consisting of pill boxes, concrete block obstacles, barbed wire, old railway lines and ditches. Twenty-seven beaches were protected with various obstacles and mines.

1940 was perhaps the worst and most anxious year of the war for the Allies. It consisted of mostly bad news such as the Battle of Narvik, the evacuation from Dunkirk and Italy's declaration of war on Britain. On top of this was the constant threat of an invasion; Britain became a nation under siege. Every effort was put in to produce and manufacture goods; people were encouraged not to waste any food, to grow as much as possible, and to re-use clothing. But Britain was still a trading nation, and therefore had to import from other countries. As during the First World War, Britain's lifeline was vulnerable to attack by enemy submarines and surface warships.

Despite the wealth of information obtained during the First World War in anti-submarine warfare, very little research was pursued during the inter-war years. In the thirties, the development of submarine detection or any new ordnance was not given the same impetus as that of Bomber Command. Coastal Command still used the standard service ordnance.

North Atlantic Convoy. (*via RN*)

The Merchantman *Protesilaus* being towed having been damaged by a mine.

The biggest threat was from the German U-boats that preyed on merchant shipping in the Atlantic, and even in the coastal waters of the British Isles.

The U-boat (*underseeboot* – the German word for submarine) was a basic diesel-electric submarine that completely changed sea warfare in the First World War and especially in the Second. As in 1914, the German High Naval Command declared that all ships in disputed waters, both commercial shipping and civilian passenger liners, were to be regarded as legitimate targets. Initially, the disputed areas included sea lanes leading to the British Isles or any country of the British Empire, but soon this extended to anywhere in the world.

At the beginning of the Second World War, Germany had fewer than 100 U-boats, but within four years it had produced several thousand. The most common type built between 1940 and 1945 was Type VII-C, which carried fourteen torpedoes in its bow and stern compartments, and was armed with an 88 mm (3 inch) naval gun on the deck near the conning tower. The type was 221 feet in length with a beam of 19 feet and a crew of forty-four sailors. The submarine's Achilles heel was that it had to surface to recharge its batteries and, therefore, became easy prey for patrolling aircraft. Later in the war, the U-boat's range was extended with the addition of a snorkel that allowed the submarine to remain underwater at periscope depth to recharge its batteries.

Initially, the submarines operated singly, but when the convoy system (merchant shipping sailing together for protection) was introduced, the U-boats began to operate in packs (Wolf Packs).

Until 1943, the U-boats dominated the sea lanes, but after the British obtained the German Enigma coding machine, scientists at Bletchley Park

A German U-boat.

Radar on the Great Orme at Llandudno. (*Conwy Archive*)

were able to decode all German Naval orders and pin point the location of the U-boat packs. Extended air cover was available with the introduction of long-range aircraft and escort carriers, and the development of new sonar and radio direction finders. Specialised anti-submarine frigates and destroyers armed with the forward firing Hedgehog and Squid anti-submarine bombs (types of mortars) were also introduced. When the war ended in 1945, German U-boats had claimed over 2,800 Allied ships, but at a cost of 784 U-boats with 28,000 men dead and 5,000 taken prisoner, out of a total strength of 40,000.

It was not only the sea lanes that were vulnerable to attacks. In the Second World War, Welsh soil was under threat from the air. The Luftwaffe launched a devastating onslaught on the United Kingdom; firstly on the airfields, followed by attacks on the towns, whether they were involved in the war effort or not. When France fell in May 1940, Wales came in the range of German bombers based on French airfields.

The Home Chain defence: Guyed transmitter masts at RAF Hayscastle Cross, Pembrokeshire. (*via Subbrit*)

The Focke Wulf FW200 Condor was also a menace to Allied shipping.

Any place or area involved in the war effort was regarded as a legitimate target. The docks at Cardiff were bombed on 12/13 September 1940. These raids were classed by the military as nuisance raids, conducted by two or three aircraft.

Of all the towns in Wales, Swansea suffered perhaps the most from enemy air raids. The first raid took place in June 1940 on the town's Kings Dock. There was a large raid on Llandarcy oil refinery on 1/2 September 1940, which caused a large fire. On the night of 17 January 1941, the docks were bombed again, with several bombs falling on the occupied part of the town, killing fifty-eight people. The heaviest raid of the war was the three-night blitz of 19–21 February 1941. In the course of 13 hours, 800 high explosive and 30,000 incendiary bombs fell on the town.

Although north Wales was classed as the safest area in the United Kingdom, it did not completely escape from the German bomber; any industrial area in any part of Wales was a prime target for the enemy. The airfield at Penrhos was bombed five times in 1940, and between 1940 and 1941, the port of Holyhead and the surrounding area was bombed twelve times. Even smaller towns and villages on the coast and in the valleys were bombed. Thankfully there were no casualties.

Pembrokeshire, especially Pembroke Dock, was subjected to several air raids between July 1940 and June 1941. The most dramatic was the bombing of Llanreath oil tanks by three enemy bombers on 17 August. The fire raged for eighteen days and the black smoke could be seen from every part of the county.

Margam Radar site.

Wooden receiver towers at Hayscastle Cross, part of the Home Chain defence. (*via Subbrit*)

It was not only the industrial parts and large towns of Wales that were bombed, but also the small villages and hamlets. Raids on local shipping and fishing boats became common until the fighter airfields became operational at Angle, Fairwood and Pembrey in south Wales, and Valley and Wrexham in north Wales (*see* Chapter 9).

From 6 July 1940, as an additional defence against enemy submarines, a flotilla of six motor patrol boats armed with depth charges was stationed in the Menai Straits. These boats were able to provide coastal escorts for shipping, especially the Irish ferries.

Other defences located around Wales were artillery units armed with 6-inch Naval QF guns, 12 pounder QF, 6 pounder, 3.7-inch and 40 mm Bofor guns. These were usually based at the various gun firing ranges like Ty Croes on Anglesey, Tonfanau near Tywyn, and Manorbier in Pembrokeshire, with their gun emplacements pointing out to sea. Other emplacements were built especially for the purpose, such as the coastal artillery training units on the Great Orme in Llandudno and on the Little Orme between Llandudno and Colwyn Bay in north Wales. The Victorian fortification on Flat Holme and Steep Holm Island in the Severn Estuary was used for coastal and anti-aircraft defence batteries. There were searchlight and gun emplacements on Mumbles Hill, Oystermouth, on the Gower. Several anti-aircraft batteries were located near towns and industrial sites as a protection against enemy bombers.

The 6-inch QF Naval gun was used in coastal defences.

A Short Sunderland circling the stricken ship, *Kensington Court.*

The Avro Anson of RAF Coastal Command escorting an incoming convoy in 1939.

Aircraft from Pembrokeshire's airfield and other bases flew up to 2,000 miles into the Atlantic to meet and escort the vital homecoming convoys, which were the country's lifeline. Coastal Command aircraft became a welcomed sight to the weary sailors who had braved enemy aircraft and U-boats in the north Atlantic. Right up to the end of the war in Europe, the Sunderlands, Liberators and Halifaxes from the county's airfields kept a watchful eye on the important sea lanes.

Wales also had other airfields which contributed in a more indirect fashion to the enemy's defeat during the Second World War. These airfields provided essential training and support to the three services. They supplied target tugs and pilotless aircraft for the army anti-aircraft gunners and Royal Navy gunners to practice on, training and aircrews for operating on Royal Navy aircraft carriers, and training for pilots in photo-reconnaissance roles.

Wales is a small nation, but it contributed a great deal to the defeat of Nazism in Europe. Not only in its sacrifice of men fighting on the continent or in the Far East, but also in its airfields and bases manned by brave and dedicated servicemen, determined to make the sea lanes around Wales and its approaches safe for shipping.

Barrage balloon unit
outside Cardiff. (*PRO*)

CHAPTER 7

Flying Boats

The only flying boat station in Wales was at Pembroke Dock, located in the sheltered bay of Milford Haven. Because of its sheltered inlet, Milford Haven has been an ideal location for military use for centuries. It has become a popular haven for ships of all sizes, and when its potential was realized, naval docks and shipbuilding were established on its banks. In the 1920s, the Haven was chosen as a flying boat station for the protection of the Western Approaches.

The flying boat base at Pembroke Dock was officially opened on 1 January 1930. It was situated on the south bank of the Haven on a small headland below Barrack Hill, opposite the town of Neyland. Expansion was limited because of nearby housing. The base was initially very basic consisting of a few wooden huts, a Blister type hangar and a wooden jetty and slipway. During the 1930s, it was gradually developed and the facilities were extended. In 1936, a new concrete slipway replaced the wooden one, and new permanent workshops, mess rooms and accommodation were built for the station's personnel. Eventually, the base was to have two modified 'B' type hangars, and a T2 hangar for storage and to accommodate a smaller type of flying boat. An elegant Georgian style Officers' Mess was built and became a landmark for miles around. By the outbreak of the Second World War, Pembroke Dock flying boat base was one of the premier flying boat stations in the United Kingdom.

The flying boat base had two daylight alighting areas, one opposite Milford Haven and the other east of the RAF station. The night alighting area consisted of flare path buoys and was located opposite Angle Bay, which was also used for beaching should the need arise. However, on a number of occasions the Coastal Artillery Search Light unit at the blockhouse at St Anne's Head was switched on to assist incoming flying boats that were in serious difficulty attempting to land.

On 1 March 1931, No. 210 Squadron was reformed as a flying boat squadron at Felixstowe, but in June it moved to Pembroke Dock to

A Sunderland of No. 210 Squadron co-operating with a RN warship searching for U-boats. (*B. Owen*)

Members of the WAAF cleaning a Catalina windscreen.

establish the new base. The squadron was equipped with Supermarine Southampton II flying boats, but was also involved in the developing trials of other types. Eventually, due to the squadron's close connection with Wales, it adopted a dragon as its badge and a Welsh motto 'Yn y nwyfre yn edfan'.

In August 1934, Pembroke Dock became the base for No. 821 Royal Naval Squadron, equipped with Fairey Seal seaplanes. No. 210 Squadron returned to Pembrokeshire in October 1935, and was re-equipped with Rangoon I flying boats. In September 1935, the squadron left Pembroke Dock but returned again with Singapore III aircraft in 1936 to be re-equipped with the brand new Short Sunderland Mk I. In July 1940, No. 210 Squadron moved to Oban, but when it returned in October 1942 it had been re-equipped with Consolidated Catalina Is.

On 1 December 1934, No. 230 Squadron was reformed at Pembroke Dock, but it did not receive its Short Singapore III flying boats until April 1935. After a brief familiarisation, the squadron moved to Aboukir and Alexandria in Egypt in September 1935. The squadron returned to Pembroke Dock in September 1936 to be re-equipped with Short Sunderland Mk I flying boats, before moving to the Far East and Africa, where it remained throughout the war. The squadron finally returned to Pembroke Dock in February 1949.

Another RAF squadron to be reformed at Pembroke Dock was No. 228 on 15 December 1936, with an interim selection of aircraft, which included one Supermarine Scapa (K7306), a Saro London (K5258), and

A Painting of a Sunderland.

two Short Singapore IIIs (K4579, K6913). The squadron received its full complement of eight Supermarine Stranrear Mk Is the following April. In September 1938, the squadron moved to Invergordon for a month, but returned to Pembroke Dock to be re-equipped with Short Sunderland Mk Is prior to their move to Kalafrana. A week after war broke out, the whole squadron returned to Pembroke Dock, where they remained until June 1940. The squadron returned again to Pembroke Dock on 4 May 1943. The Sunderlands were flown direct from Lough Erne to the Haven and the ground crew and other personnel were flown in Horsa gliders towed by Albemarle's bombers to Talbenny, escorted by the Sunderlands. No. 228 Squadron remained at Pembroke Dock until the unit was disbanded on 4 June 1945.

The Short Sunderland was the Royal Air Force Coastal Command's main long-range flying boat during the Second World War. The aircraft entered service pre-war, and remained in service well into the early fifties. It was used for patrol work, anti-submarine duties, convoy escort, search and rescue, and transport.

The Sunderland's first flight was from Short's factory at Rochester, Kent, on 6 October 1937, and entered service with the Royal Air Force the following year on 28 May 1938. It was developed from the famous Short 'C' class flying boat, which had opened up air routes to the Middle East, the Far East, West Africa, and Australia with Imperial Airways in the early

Leading up to the outbreak of war, Coastal Command operated several types of biplane flying boats. This photograph shows a Stranrear of No. 208 Squadron taking off.

A battle-weary Sunderland on patrol.

A Short Sunderland escorting a convoy in 1939.

1930s. As the war progressed, enemy aircraft began to treat the Sunderland with a great deal of respect, as from the Mk III onwards they were armed with up to fourteen .303-inch machine guns and two .50-inch Browning machine guns. The aircraft soon became to be known by German pilots as 'Das Fliegende Stachelschwein' – 'The Flying Porcupines'.

The Sunderland became a 'Jack of all trades' in RAF service; because of its huge size and versatility it was also used for VIP transport, troop carrying, and search and rescue. It served with a total of twenty squadrons in the Royal Air Force Coastal Command in every theatre of operations, but it was during the Battle of the Atlantic that the flying boat became a legend.

Between 1938 and 1947, eleven operational Sunderland squadrons were stationed at Pembroke Dock; some were permanently based there while others were on detachments, re-equipping or on exercise. The squadrons were Nos 10, 95, 119, 201, 204, 210, 228, 230, 422, 461, and 4 OTU (Operational Training Unit), which was often used operationally.

The Sunderland was perhaps the most important asset Coastal Command had in its fight against the German U-boat. The following paragraphs deal with some of the exploits and bravery of the crews of various squadrons while based at Pembroke Dock.

The first casualty after the declaration of war was Sunderland L2165, which crash landed off Dale on 17 September 1939. As soon as No. 228 Squadron returned to Pembroke Dock at the outbreak of war, it was involved with anti-submarine patrol and convoy duties in the Atlantic. The squadron's first encounter with the enemy took place on 9 September 1939, followed on 14 September by Sunderland L2167 attacking the U-boat that sank the merchantman, SS *Vancouver City*. The Sunderland circled the lifeboats until the occupants were rescued by another ship.

A Short Sunderland of No. 210 Squadron meeting an inbound troop convoy south of Ireland. (*B. Owen*)

The following day, Sunderland N6135 sunk during a landing accident; it was eventually beached but the damage was beyond repair and it was broken up for spares. On the 18 September, the squadron was again in action when the SS *Kensington Court*, a 4,900 ton merchant ship, was shelled and sunk by U-boats. Various patrolling Sunderlands picked up a distress signal, three of which were from No. 228 Squadron. Sunderland N9025, piloted by Flight Lieutenant Thurston N. W. Smith (who had been with the squadron since June 1938), was first to arrive on the scene, by which time the U-boat had departed, leaving the survivors clinging to anything that would float. Flight Lieutenant Smith landed his aircraft near the stricken ship and rescued twenty of the survivors. By now, the aircraft was dangerously overloaded, but with sheer skill he managed to take off. Another Sunderland from RAF Mount Batten arrived on the scene and rescued the remainder of the ship's crew. Both aircraft returned to their respective bases and both pilots received the DFC (Distinguished Flying Cross) for their exploits.

On 21 October 1939, a Sunderland (N9025) commanded by Flight Lieutenant Brooks made an unsuccessful attack on a U-boat. During the month, No. 228 Squadron had made a total of thirty-five sorties, mostly convoy escorts. In December 1939, the squadron's commanding officer made an attack on a submarine, followed in January by Flight Lieutenant Brooks on another U-boat.

On 1 June 1940, No. 320 (Dutch) Squadron was formed at Pembroke Dock, composed of personnel of the Royal Netherlands Naval Air Service who had escaped from occupied Holland and brought with them a

A Pembroke Dock-based Sunderland of No. 201 Squadron on Atlantic patrol, June 1944. (*S. Broomfields*)

Servicing a Fokker TVIII of No. 320 (Dutch) Squadron at Pembroke Dock. (*R. Neth, AF Archives*)

collection of twenty-six aircraft. Nine seaplanes, eight Fokker T-VIIIWs and one C-XIVW became the nucleus of the squadron. The squadron was soon operational, carrying out convoy patrols and anti-shipping sorties in the South-Western Approaches. During these sorties, two crews were lost and the squadron became non-operational because of the lack of spares. In August, the unit was re-equipped with Avro Ansons and based at Carew.

No. 240 Squadron was based at Pembroke Dock between May and July 1940. It was equipped with Supermarine Stranrear flying boats under the command of Wing Commander A. W. Bates. Ironically, one of the squadron's Stranrears was scrambled when the airfield at Carew was bombed on 17 July.

In January 1941, No. 95 Squadron was formed at Pembroke Dock under the command of Wing Commander F. J. Freeanges, and was equipped with seven Short Sunderland Mk Is. After a brief crew familiarisation, the squadron was posted to Free Town in South Africa, where it patrolled the sea lanes around the southern tip of Africa and remained there until the end of the war.

No. 4 Operational Training Unit (OTU) was another Sunderland squadron formed and based at Pembroke Dock. The unit was formed in March 1941 to train crews on flying boats, and remained at the base until

Short Sunderland Mk I of No. 95 Squadron at Pembroke Dock.

Personnel of No. 10 Squadron playing rugby in between sorties. (*Australian Archives*)

it was disbanded in April 1951. During its time at Pembroke Dock, the unit operated various types of flying boats: Supermarine Stranrears, Saro London IIs, Lerwicks Is, Catalina Is, and Short Sunderland Is, IIs, and Vs.

On 1 June 1941, No. 10 RAAF (Royal Australian Air Force) Squadron Sunderlands returned to Pembroke Dock. The squadron was formed towards the end of 1939, and was the only RAAF unit operating in the United Kingdom that did not adopt RAF squadron numbers. On 1 February 1940, the squadron was declared operational and was posted on 1 April to Mount Batten, Plymouth. The Australians were soon in action; during a patrol one of its aircraft was attacked by two Arado seaplanes, one was shot down the other was driven off. On 30 June, two patrolling Sunderlands were attacked by two enemy Fw200s in the Bay of Biscay vicinity.

Another unit, No. 119 Squadron, was formed at Pembroke Dock under the command of Squadron Leader N. Williamson, and equipped with Sunderland Mk Is. It moved to Lough Erne in April 1942, where it was re-equipped with Consolidated Catalina flying boats. The squadron returned to Pembroke Dock in August 1942 to be equipped with the new Sunderland Mk IIIs, but due to a shortage of trained aircrews, the unit was

A tail view of a Sunderland of No. 10 Australian Squadron. (*Australian Archives*)

Sunderland ML839 of No. 10 (Australian) Squadron on patrol.

disbanded on 17 April 1943. Most of its crew and aircraft were transferred to either No. 461 Squadron or No. 4 Operational Training Unit. During its short stay at Pembroke Dock, the unit completed several patrol sorties in the Channel and the Bay of Biscay.

In May 1943, the battle against submarines peaked when Sunderlands sank five U-boats and seriously damaged another two. Sunderland tactics were usually focused on spotting a U-boat, then radar or visual lined up the attack to cross the submarines track above the conning tower or its periscope wake. Four or six depth charges would be dropped, three landing on either side of the submarine, crushing it in between the explosion before it had time to submerge. The tactic was successful in the majority of attacks.

During the D-Day landings, Coastal Command was given a special mission, code name Operation Cork, to close the entrances to the English Channel. A series of overlapping patrols in conjunction with the Royal Navy were conducted to keep all U-boats away. The Sunderlands and other Coastal Command aircraft flew at 1,000 feet in a designated box patrol of 60 miles by 15 miles, which usually took approximately an hour and half. The aircraft would continue to fly the box for up to 14 hours, until relieved by another aircraft. As a number of crew remarked, it was very monotonous, but it worked.

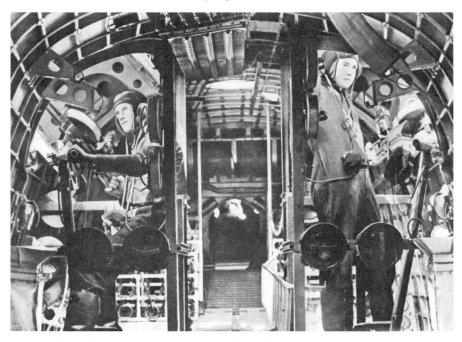

Two midship observers on watch in a Sunderland.

On 30 May 1943, Catalina JX264, belonging to No. 210 Squadron, was badly damaged by U-boat anti-aircraft cannons. With one crewman dead, the flying boat limped back to the safety of the Haven, but after an emergency landing the badly holed fuselage sank just after the crew had managed to get clear. The squadron was disbanded at Hamworthy Junction in December 1943, but was reformed by renumbering No. 190 Squadron at Sullom Voe. However, a detachment of the squadron's Catalinas was stationed at Pembroke Dock from January 1944 to June 1945.

When No. 228 Squadron returned to Wales in May 1943, it was again involved in patrolling the Western Approaches and the Bay of Biscay. The squadron sorties rate went up, and before long the casualties rate also increased. Two Sunderlands and their crews were reported missing, but Flight Lieutenant French is credited with destroying one U-boat. Aircraft and crew losses mounted during June and July, and to replace the losses at least two new Sunderlands were flown in each week. The squadron U-boat tally continued to increase with at least two enemy submarines sunk. Three more successful attacks followed in August, including the destruction of U-383, sunk by Flight Lieutenant S. White of No. 228 Squadron, and U-106, sunk by Flight Officer R. D. Hanbury of No. 228 Squadron and Flight Lieutenant I. A. F. Clarke of No. 461 Squadron.

SARO at Beaumaris converted the Catalinas for Coastal Command; this included fitting Leigh-Lights. (*BHC*)

U-106 being attacked by two Sunderlands of Nos 208 and 461 Squadrons from Pembroke Dock. (*National Archives of Canada*)

No. 461 RAAF Squadron was another of Pembroke Dock's busy Sunderland units. On 2 May 1943, Flight Lieutenant E. C. Smith sank U-332 after a fairly short encounter. On 2 June, during a long patrol in the Bay of Biscay, two Junkers Ju88s and two Focke Wulf Fw190s, and later a further eight Junkers Ju88s, attacked Flight Lieutenant Colin Walker's Sunderland (EJ134). After continuous pounding by cannon and machine gun shells, the Sunderland was so badly damaged that its instruments were not functioning; the port outer engine was out of action and the hydraulic system to the gun turrets was damaged. Only the manually operated guns could be used. The rear gunner was wounded and one of the waist gunners was dead, but in spite of their dilemma, three of the attacking Ju88s were shot down.

Due to the condition of the aircraft and the crew, Flight Lieutenant Walker decided to break off the engagement and head for safety. There was no chance of reaching Pembroke Dock, as it was nearly 300 miles away; the only solution was to make for the nearest British coastline. Flight Lieutenant Walker managed to land the damaged flying boat 300 yards off Pra Sands near Marazian, Cornwall, running her aground in shallow water before she could sink. For this gallantry and airmanship, Flight Lieutenant Walker was awarded the DSO while his second pilot Flight Officer W. J. Dowling received a DFC. Two others were awarded the DFM, and a fourth was mentioned in despatches.

Engineers working on the Sunderland's Pegasus engines.

On 29 May 1943, Sunderland T9114 'E' of No. 461 Squadron, piloted by Gordon Singleton, an Australian, made a dry landing at Angle airfield. The Sunderland had taken off from Pembroke Dock that morning to rescue a downed Sunderland (JM675) which had crashed due to enemy action. Because of heavy seas, Singleton decided to pass the rescued crew to a French sloop and was advised not to attempt taking off in the heavy swell. During a take off in heavy weather the aircraft sustained extensive damage to the fuselage and a landing on water was regarded too dangerous. As Angle was the nearest airfield, the pilot headed there and with great skill landed the large flying boat without any casualties. After a close inspection, the Sunderland was deemed beyond repair and was dismantled and transported by road to Pembroke Dock.

Two months later, on 30 July 1943, No. 461 Squadron Sunderlands were again in action. This time they were joined by a RAF Liberator and a Halifax as well as a USN Liberator in an attack on three surfaced U-boats. The aircraft were kept at bay by the heavy flak put up by the submarines, until the Halifax managed to score a direct hit on one of them, resulting in its sinking. Meanwhile, a No. 461 Sunderland, piloted by Flight Lieutenant Dudley Morrows, dived through a barrage of flak from 37 mm and 20 mm cannons, put up by the remaining U-boats, and dropped its depth charges on U-461, cutting the submarine in half. Despite the other U-boats continuing to put up a barrage of anti-aircraft fire, Morrows returned and dropped a life dinghy for the U-461 survivors.

On his homeward return to Pembroke Dock, Flight Lieutenant Morrows spotted a lone U-boat on the surface which he attacked with machine gun fire and depth charges, but without any success. By this time his aircraft was badly damaged due to the relentless flak put up by the submarines, and was running low on fuel. Morrows nursed the Sunderland back to friendly shores, but as there was no chance of returning to Pembroke Dock he made an emergency landing near St Mary's in the Scillies.

Two weeks later, Flight Lieutenant Morrows was again in action; while patrolling in his Sunderland just off the Spanish coast, he was attacked by six Luftwaffe Ju88s. After a fierce fight, the enemy broke off, but the Sunderland was badly damaged. Having great difficulty keeping the flying boat airborne, Morrows had no choice but to ditch the aircraft. A Royal Navy destroyer picked up all the crew safely the following day.

On 2 August 1943, Flight Officer R. D. Hanbury spotted and sank U-106 on his return from a patrol. But, like all the squadrons based at Pembroke Dock, No. 461 Squadron had its list of casualties. On 13 August, Wing Commander Halliday, the squadron's commanding officer, was killed attempting to land in a heavy swell in an effort to rescue the crew of a ditched Wellington which had been involved in a clash with a Focke Wulf Fw200 Condor. Only one of the Sunderland's crew survived.

A United States Naval squadron, VP63, equipped with Catalinas, made a brief appearance in 1943. The unit made several patrols and anti-submarine sweeps in the Bay of Biscay and the Western Approaches before being posted to Port Leyautey in North Africa in December 1943. Most of the aircrew joined USN 4th and 9th Squadrons of 479 Anti-Submarine Group, equipped with Consolidated PB4Y-1 Liberators, at Dunkeswell, Devon.

By December 1943, No. 228 Squadron was flying sixty-four anti-submarine sorties a month from Pembroke Dock. During January 1944, it lost three crews through enemy action and aircraft failures. The squadron made very few contacts until June, when a number of squadrons were involved in bottling up the western end of the Channel, ready for the invasion.

No. 201 Squadron arrived at Pembroke Dock in March 1944, and was immediately involved with pre-occupation sweeps in the English Channel, protecting the invasion fleets. No. 201 Squadron Sunderlands made two notable U-boat attacks in June. One successful encounter by Flight Lieutenant Baveystock sank an enemy submarine, but the other caused the loss of Squadron Leader Ruth and his crew. However, the following month the squadron was again in action in the Channel, when Flight Lieutenant Walters' Sunderland attacked and sank another U-boat. On 18 August 1944, Flight Lieutenant Baveystock scored his third kill. The squadron was based at Pembroke Dock during these four months, and its aircraft

A total of 310 Catalinas passed through Beaumaris. This photograph shows aircraft moored in the Menai Straits. (*BHC*)

A magnificent view of two Sunderlands of No. 201 Squadron taking off from
Pembroke Dock.

were involved in several encounters with German submarines and surface
ships.

On 7 June 1944, Flight Lieutenant C. G. D. Lancaster of No. 228
Squadron sank U-970 with a combination of bombs and depth charges.
Four days later, Flight Lieutenant M. E. Slaughter attacked and damaged
U-333. Several more successful attacks were made on U-boats during
proceeding months.

There were two Canadian Sunderland units based at Pembroke Dock,
Nos 422 and 423 Squadrons. The former was based in the Haven between
November 1944 and July 1945, and was involved in a flurry of anti-
submarine activity in the Channel and Bay of Biscay between 5 and 8
March 1945. The unit's Sunderlands made several depth charge attacks on
enemy U-boats, but after that the squadron began to run down. On 2 July
1945, the squadron left Pembroke Dock to reform as a Liberator bomber
squadron, part of the Tiger Force, a very long-range bomber group intended
for operation against the mainland of Japan. The reformation, however,
never took place, and the squadron was disbanded on 3 September 1945.

No. 423 Squadron (RCAF) was heavily involved in the U-boat's last
exploits in the English Channel. The squadron's Sunderlands were credited
with the last U-boat fight of the war on 4 May 1945.

A total of thirty-six enemy U-boats were sunk in the Second World
War by RAF Coastal Command Sunderlands. It was not surprising that a
base as important as Pembroke Dock attracted the attention of Luftwaffe

bombers. There were a number of raids on the ports, the fuel storage tanks, and other military installations in the Haven area. Because of its close proximity, several bombs landed on the RAF station. None of the moored flying boats were damaged but one land mine hit the base, causing some damage and killing an airman. Land mines were often dropped to cause damage later, after the raid. The town received a number of hits causing severe damage and a number of casualties.

In 1945, most of the Pembroke Dock Sunderland squadrons were disbanded, and the Australian and Canadian personnel returned home to their own countries. Only Nos 201 and 230 Squadrons, together with No. 4 OTU (later to be renamed as No. 235 OCU), remained at the base. The last Sunderland was officially withdrawn from RAF service in February 1957, when No. 208 Squadron was disbanded at Pembroke Dock.

The other flying boat station in Wales was Beaumaris, situated on the Menai Straits, which provided an ideal anchorage and operating area for the flying boats.

Although Beamaris was not directly involved with anti-submarine and convoy patrol operations, its presence was nevertheless important as it supplied and modified aircraft to be used by Coastal Command. No doubt, with its aircraft test flying in the area, it deterred many a U-boat from harassing ships in Conwy Bay and around the coast of Anglesey and north Wales.

The station was operated by Saunders Roe (SARO), who had been given the contract to anglicise the Consolidated PBY 5 Catalina flying boat, imported from the United States for the Royal Air Force. At Beaumaris,

Another flying boat evaluated was the Martin Mariner, seen here parked in front of Friars at Beaumaris. (*BHC*)

Intended as replacements for the Sunderland, several Coronados were acquired from the States.

the Catalinas were fitted with British components, including .303-inch machine guns, standard British bomb racks, RAF Communications, ASV radar and Leigh lights, bringing them up to Coastal Command's specifications. The first Catalina (AM267) arrived on 15 April 1941, piloted by Group Captain Cahill. Up until 1945, SARO modified a total of 310 Catalinas. Between 1943 and 1944, eleven Coronados and six Mariners were evaluated at Beaumaris as possible replacements for the Sunderlands and Catalinas, but were found unsuitable and unsafe and were used only for transport. In 1944, several Sunderlands were sent by Short Bros at Belfast for minor modifications and upgrading before their onward flight to Mount Batten and Pembroke Dock.

CHAPTER 8

Coastal Command Land-Based Aircraft

Coastal Command began the Second World War with one important advantage which had been lacking in the First War. It had been fully mobilised in August 1939, prior to the outbreak of hostilities. The Admiralty and Royal Air Force carried out extensive exercises to test the response of Coastal Command and Royal Navy warships to enemy threats to shipping and the coast line. Many air patrols were conducted in the North Sea, the English Channel, and the Western Approaches. When war was declared in September 1939, there was the added element of air power; something that had only come into existence towards the end of the First World War.

The Royal Air Force showed no enthusiasm to develop any special land-based aircraft for either anti-submarine warfare or for convoy escort, except flying boats. As a result, coastal defences were allowed to stagnate. The Admiralty was also slow in developing any sort of coastal patrol boats to provide protection for coastal shipping; in 1939, they did recommend the establishment of coastal reconnaissance units, but nothing materialised. From the very beginning, the Admiralty introduced the convoy system, which proved successful in the First World War, but it had to be protected by warships and aircraft.

To meet the menace of the U-boat, Coastal Command had at its immediate disposal five flying boat, seven Anson and two Vildebeest squadrons. A Hudson squadron was also in the process of being formed. On the day the war broke out, there were only 171 aircraft available with trained crews. The area of protection covered was limited by the range of the aircraft. Flying boats from Pembroke Dock (*see* Chapter 7) covered the farthest points from their bases, while the land-based aircraft patrolled around 100 miles from base.

Coastal Command had always been the Cinderella of the service; its land-based aircraft had always been passed on from Bomber Command. At the outbreak of the war, the command consisted of a collection of

The Vickers Vildebeest was the main Coastal Command aircraft in the 1930s.

obsolescent light aircraft for submarine spotting: Naval Swordfish, Austers, Vincents, Tiger Moths, Lysanders, Rapides etc. The Command's main twin-engine aircraft during those early years was the Avro Anson, although several twin-engine Lockheed Hudson aircraft were ordered from the United States. The main Coastal Command bases in Wales were initially the flying boat station of Pembroke Dock and Carew Cheriton airfield, which provided support with land-based aircraft. They were both located in Pembrokeshire.

In the Second World War, the main tasks of the RAF Coastal Command, operating from Pembrokeshire and the West Country, were to fly U-boat patrols over the Bay of Biscay and to protect convoys in the Western Approaches. The Command flew mostly flying boats from bases like Pembroke Dock and Mount Batten, but because of the serious threat to the convoys, the life lines of the islands, several Bomber Command squadrons were eventually transferred to convoy duties.

When war broke out, there was only one airfield in south Wales capable of operating aircraft for coastal protection, and that was Carew Cheriton in Pembrokeshire. Carew was built on the site of the former First World War airship station at Milton, RNAS Pembroke, which operated aircraft and airships against enemy submarines. Prior to the arrival of permanent Coastal Command units, the resident aircraft at the airfield were DH Tiger Moths and Hornet Moths belonging to No. 5 Coastal Patrol Flight, which was formed at the airfield on 1 March 1940.

An Avro Anson of No. 206 Squadron.

The object of patrol flights was to protect coastal shipping and spot submarines loitering around the coast. The presence of an aircraft, even a small biplane such as a Moth, made it impossible for U-boats to travel on the surface in daylight. The area covered by No. 5 Coastal Patrol Flight was from Bideford Bay to Carmarthen Bay, as well as the southern coast of the county. Usually, aircraft would patrol in pairs, each pair with sections of the coastline or area to cover. As the pilots were local, they had a great advantage of knowing the coast, but still several false sightings were reported, which were investigated further by Ansons based at Carew. The Tiger Moths and Hornet Moths had an endurance of up to two hours and petrol capacity of 14 gallons. No. 5 Coastal Patrol Flight was disbanded on 27 May 1940, and its aircraft were used by other training and communication units.

In August 1939, the first Coastal Command unit arrived at Carew airfield in the form of a detachment of seven Avro Anson Mk Is of 'C' Flight, No. 217 Squadron, from RAF Warmwell, Dorset. On 16 September 1939, 'C' Flight was supplemented by a detachment of six Avro Ansons from No. 206 Squadron, RAF Bircham Newton. Both units were involved in coastal and shipping patrols in the Bristol Channel and Irish Sea. While based at Carew, only one positive encounter was recorded, and that was by an Anson of No. 206 Squadron on 20 September 1939 off Lundey Island. Returning after a patrol, the Anson spotted the coning tower of a U-boat and dropped two 100 lb anti-submarine bombs, but without any effect, and the submarine disappeared beneath the waves. The 100 lb anti-

Avro Ansons flying convoy escort in early 1940.

submarine bombs were the standard ordnance used at the time, but had a very low lethal radius and had to be exploded within 10 feet of the target to cause any serious damage.

In May 1940, members of the Royal Netherlands Naval Air Service arrived at Carew in a collection of twenty-six land and water-based aircraft. The aircrew had escaped from Holland when German forces invaded the country. The Fokker seaplanes T-VIIIW remained at Pembroke Dock, while the land-based aircraft were attached to the airfield at Carew to form the basis of No. 320 Squadron. Due to the lack of spares for the Fokker aircraft, it was decided to re-equip the squadron with British-built aircraft. After familiarisation and training on borrowed Avro Anson Mk Is, the Dutch Naval unit received its own aircraft. The second Dutch unit, No. 321 Squadron, was formed on 1 June 1940, equipped with Avro Ansons. Within a month, both units were ready to partake in the Irish Sea patrols. On one such patrol on 9 August 1940, Anson KG6235 suffered technical problems flying over Carmarthen Bay and was forced to land on Pendine Sands; it struck an anti-invasion obstacle and was severely damaged. The crew managed to wade ashore before the aircraft was totally submerged in the soft sand and the incoming tide.

With the fall of France, ports used by the Germans became targets for RAF Coastal Command. Seeking and destroying U-boats was still its main

An Avro Anson of No. 320 (Dutch) Squadron at Carew. (*R. Neth, AF Archives*)

objective, but attacks were also made on enemy shipping in occupied Europe. For this purpose, on 21 March 1941, No. 236 Squadron arrived from St Eval, equipped with eleven Bristol Blenheim IVs and seven Bristol Beaufighter ICs. They remained at Carew until February 1942. A detachment from No. 500 Squadron, equipped with Bristol Blenheim Mk IVs, was based at Carew from 30 May 1941 to 22 March 1942 to attack shipping targets on the Brest Peninsular. While at Carew, the detachment was re-equipped with Lockheed Hudson Mk I aircraft, which had just arrived from the States.

Due to the attention the airfield received from German bombers in the early part of 1941, a detachment of Hawker Hurricane Mk Is from Nos 32 and 238 Squadrons were sent to Carew from Pembrey. The fighters remained at the airfield from April 1941 to June 1941, and were not once called to defend the base, although they were occasionally scrambled on a false alarm. They did, however, provide an escort to patrolling aircraft and coastal shipping.

On 22 October 1941, No. 254 Squadron detached three Bristol Beaufighters from RAF Bircham Newton to provide a long-range escort for seven Bristol Blenheims, which had already arrived from Aldergrove, Northern Ireland. These aircraft were to take part in convoy duty in the Irish Sea, which U-boats and enemy land-based aircraft had rendered a great problem for Allied shipping. Several skirmishes took place between Carew's aircraft and German Focke Wulf Fw200 Condors and Junkers Ju88s over the Irish Sea, but no enemy aircraft were reported as being

Crew preparing a Bristol Blenheim IV for patrol. (*via Lloyd Evans*)

A Bristol Blenheim IVF of No. 254 Squadron.

Coastal Patrol Flight at Carew in early 1940.

shot down. On a number of occasions, the Beaufighter was mistaken by the Germans for a twin-engine bomber, which proved devastating for the enemy.

No. 236 Squadron's Beaufighters were also involved in reconnaissance flights over Brest from their forward base at St Eval. On one such flight on 19 December 1941, Sergeant Mooney and Sergeant Phillips were both awarded the Distinguished Flying Medal (DFM) for their brave exploit. The squadron's other duties were escorting BOAC Douglas DC-3 flights from Lisbon to Chivenor or Whitchurch, and the Irish Mail steamer sailings into the port of Goodwick, Fishguard.

When two new Pembrokeshire airfields became operational at Talbenny and Dale, Carew airfield was reverted primarily to a training base with a supporting role for the flying boat station at Pembroke Dock.

Talbenny airfield, situated near the village of the same name on an escarpment overlooking St Brides Bay, was officially opened on 1 May 1942, under No. 19 Group RAF Coastal Command. Its satellite, a quarter mile from the small seaside village of Dale, became operational on 1 June 1942. To the north of Dale airfield is the village of Marloes, and to the south is the scenic St Anne's head with its lighthouse. At last, Coastal Command had two prominent coastal airfields for land-based aircraft, which were in the right location and beneficial to patrols in the Bay of Biscay and the Western Approaches.

The first full squadron to be based at Talbenny was No. 311 (Czech) bomber squadron. It arrived on 12 June 1942 from RAF Aldergrove,

Line up of Wellingtons of No. 311 Squadron at Talbenny.

Northern Ireland, under Wing Commander Sanajdr DFC, who had only been transferred to coastal duties in April 1942. The squadron was equipped with eighteen Vickers Wellington Mk ICs; a formidable weapon with a top speed of 255 mph, an operational range of over 2,000 miles, and a carrying capacity of 2,000 lbs of bombs.

In June, U-boats had sunk nearly 700,300 tons of Allied shipping, but within a matter of weeks No. 311 Squadron was operational and its aircraft were flying continuous anti-submarine patrols in the Bay of Biscay area. Like most sea patrols, theirs were long and arduous with only few contacts, but the threat of long-range enemy aircraft was always present.

No. 311 Squadron's first recorded encounter with an enemy submarine was on 27 July 1942, when Squadron Leader J. Stansky, piloting Wellington DV664 'A' for Alpha, sighted and attacked U-106 which was damaged. On another flight on 6 August 1942, after hours of patient patrolling, Wellington 'P' for Papa sighted and attacked a U-boat with depth charges and .303-inch machine gun fire from the front turret, but the U-boat's destruction was unconfirmed. The squadron's first confirmed 'kill' was on 10 August 1942, by Flying Officer Nyvt, in HF922, who sank U-578.

In late August 1942, No. 311 Squadron celebrated their second anniversary as an RAF squadron; to commemorate the event the squadron was inspected by members of the exiled Czech government. They included the Czech Minister of National Defence, Mr Masaryk, the Czech Foreign Minister, and the Czech Deputy Prime Minister who had flown in an Anson the day before.

No. 311 (Czech) Squadron Wellingtons, based at Talbenny airfield.

A Wellington of No. 304 Squadron at Dale.

The Luftwaffe made a great effort to oppose Coastal Command patrols in the Bay of Biscay; formations of four or more German fighters were often reported in the vicinity.

The first squadron to be based at Dale was No. 304 (Polish) Squadron on 15 June 1942, equipped with fifteen Vickers Wellington Mk ICs and three Mk X bombers from Tiree in Scotland. No. 304 Squadron had just completed a year of operations over Germany prior to its transfer to Coastal Command, and came at a crucial time in the Battle of the Atlantic.

No. 304 Squadron's first operation took place on 30 June 1943, when six Wellingtons made an anti-submarine sweep in the Bishops Rock area, but without any success. The next operation was in the Bay of Biscay area on 10 July, when seven aircraft were on an anti-submarine reconnaissance patrol. Aircraft 'T' for Tommy spotted a surfaced U-boat, which it attacked, dropping four depth charges on the target, but a sinking was not confirmed. On 27 July 1942, No. 304 Squadron was again in action; this time a Wellington attacked an Arado AR 196 floatplane during a patrol. Unfortunately, due to low fuel, the Wellington had to break off the attack, but the enemy aircraft was seen leaving the vicinity with smoke trailing from its engine. A combined operation took place on 25 August, when all available aircraft of Nos 311 (Talbenny) and 304 Squadrons from Dale made high level bombing attacks on German tankers and harbour installations in La Pallice. Several tankers and installations were left blazing and all the aircraft returned safely to their individual bases.

Bad weather was always a problem on the Pembrokeshire coast; a typical example was an incident that occurred on 12 August 1942, when

In June 1942, No. 304 (Polish) Squadron, equipped with Wellington Mk ICs, were allocated to Coastal Command.

Anson of No. 220 Squadron that came to grief at Penrhos.

The Italian submarine *Reginaldo Guilian* being attacked by Wellingtons of No. 304 Squadron from Dale, led by Flight Officer M. Kudiorski. (*IWM*)

high winds and heavy rain were blowing across the airfield. The runway into the wind was unserviceable, so all aircraft had to use the north/south runway. During take-off, Wellington HX384 of No. 304 (Polish) Squadron failed to get airborne in the crosswind and disappeared over the cliff edge. After hectic efforts to get to the stricken plane, the Wellington and its crew disappeared under the rough seas. Sea birds were also a great problem, as was the case for most coastal airfields. They caused several incidents, mostly minor, but there were a few serious ones resulting in fatalities.

It was not only German U-boats that were hunted; the odd Italian submarine was also targeted. The *Reginaldo Guiliani*, which had sunk four Allied merchant vessels, was attacked by two Sunderlands of No. 10 Squadron from Mount Batten on 1 September 1942. The submarine suffered only slight damage, although the Captain, standing on the bridge at the time of the attack, was seriously wounded. The submarine made for Santander in Spain, but was spotted the following day by Flight Officer M. Kucharski of No. 304 Squadron in a Wellington Mk IC (HF894). Kucharski dropped six depth charges; one hit the deck but failed to explode, while others fell close to the hull causing severe damage. Another attack was made dropping two 250 lb bombs which missed the target. After another five machine gun attacks, the Wellington broke off the engagement and returned to Dale. The *Reginaldo Guiliani* reached the safety of Santander where it was repaired, but it was never again a threat to Allied shipping.

The Wellington was a very robust design. On a number of occasions it was able to limp back to base when other aircraft crashed. One such example happened on 16 September 1942, when 'E' for Ella took off from Dale on a routine daylight patrol in the Bay of Biscay, but was attacked by six Junkers Ju88s at 1612 hours. The lone Wellington became easy prey for the enemy fighters, but still managed to shoot down two Ju88s. 'E' for Ella was badly damaged with several 6-inch holes in its starboard fuel tank, a ruptured oil tank pouring oil everywhere, and a starboard engine so shot up that it had to be shut down. To make situation even more intolerable, the fuselage was full of arid black smoke. The aircraft did not have sufficient fuel to reach Dale so it had to try to land at Portreath in Cornwall. With enough fuel to make just one attempt, the pilot, Flight Officer Targowski, made a faultless landing at 1750 hours, having been airborne for over eight hours. For his gallant exploits, Targowski was awarded the Distinguished Flying Cross. Sadly, a month later, Targowski and his crew failed to return from another Bay of Biscay patrol.

In early September, Wellington 'A' for Alpha was attacked by two enemy Arado 196 floatplanes. The aircraft was badly shot up, but because of its unique construction it managed to limp back to Talbenny with a badly wounded rear gunner.

Due to constant threat and harassment by enemy aircraft during the anti-shipping raids, Coastal Command posted detachments of Bristol Beaufighter ICs from Nos 235 and 248 Squadrons to Talbenny on 5 December. Their primary job was to escort Wellington bomber strikes into enemy territory. The detachments remained at the airfield until January/February 1943, during which time no enemy aircraft came near the Wellingtons, although three Ju88s were shot down by separate patrols. The Beaufighters also patrolled the coastline for any sea disturbances associated with a submerged vessel, and carried out offensive missions against enemy shipping. The Beaufighter's armament of four 20 mm cannons and machine guns proved deadly against soft-skinned submarines and shipping.

No. 311 Squadron was again in action in November 1942 when its Wellington bombers took part in anti-shipping strikes off the Girande Estuary. These strikes were successful as several enemy ships were damaged and had to return to port for protection. In November, it was joined by its sister unit, No. 304 Squadron from Dale, while work was in progress to install a Drem lighting system at the airfield.

Night landings had always been a problem and had caused numerous accidents. Many airfields had come up with their own attempts of solving the problems, but the system that was eventually adopted was based on a home-made scheme developed at Drem airfield, east of Edinburgh. It was designated as Airfield Lighting Mark 1, but came to be commonly known as Drem Lighting, and was so successful that it was installed on

The crew of No. 304 Squadron discuss a sortie.

most active airfields. The system was comprised of three items: the runway lighting, the approach lighting and the outer circle lighting. The whole system was controlled by one switch for each runway approach, therefore on a standard three runway airfield there were only six switches controlling the complete lighting system.

While at Talbenny, the squadrons received additional Wellington GRVIIIs, and the other ICs were modified to GRVIII standard, which was more suitable for patrol work. During a patrol on 29 December 1942, aircraft of No. 311 Squadron spotted the *Regent Lion*, a tanker without a crew, adrift south of Ireland. The tanker had been abandoned seventeen days earlier after sustaining a torpedo hit and catching fire. Its position was reported and two naval tugs were sent to the scene to assess the damage and, if possible, tow the ship with its valuable cargo to a safe port.

By the end of 1942, No. 304 Squadron alone had flown 549 sorties, nearly 4,500 flying hours. On 26 January 1943, Nos 304 and 311 Squadrons conducted a joint strike against shipping in Bordeaux Harbour with sixteen Wellingtons. Several enemy ships were either sunk or damaged. For the next few months, both squadrons flew convoy escorts, bombing operations against German occupied ports in France, general reconnaissance duties, and U-boat patrols, which constantly involved skirmishes with German Junkers Ju88s. In this period, No. 304 Squadron lost two Wellingtons on operations and one in an accident over St Brides Bay. While based at Dale, No. 304 Squadron had dropped 78,000 lbs of bombs and depth charges, and attacked at least nine U-boats. Tragically, twenty-four crew members were killed or reported missing during this time. After spending another winter at Dale, No. 304 Squadron left in March 1943 for Docking in Norfolk. In May 1943, the shipping strikes came to an end and No. 311 Squadron left Talbenny to return to Bomber Command to carry out raids on Germany.

The Coastal Command Development Unit arrived at Dale from Tain in April 1943, and used Talbenny as a satellite. Although it was not directly involved in anti-shipping or anti-submarine operations, it was nevertheless an important non-operational unit within the Command and vital for keeping the sea lanes open. It was tasked with developing and training crews in the latest anti-submarine tactics and evaluating new, sophisticated equipment. It operated a diverse fleet of aircraft including Wellingtons, Whitleys, Ansons, Beauforts, Venturas, Halifaxes, and Warwicks. The CCDU was joined by No. 303 Ferry Training Unit from Talbenny for a few weeks while the airfield's lighting system was upgraded. Authors tend to ignore such units as they were not directly involved in U-boat activities, having only secondary and supporting roles, but without the development of aircraft and equipment the Battle of the Atlantic would have been lost.

A No. 320 Squadron Avro Anson on patrol over the Pembrokeshire coastline. (*R. Neth, AF Archives*)

The next phase in RAF Coastal Command's fight against the U-boats and surface shipping was the building of two more new airfields in Pembrokeshire, to operate the four new engine bombers entering the Command. The first airfield was established at St David's, a mile from the little fishing village of Solva, and just off the A487 Haverfordwest to St David's road. Its satellite airfield was situated three miles away at Brawdy. Construction of the airfield took place throughout 1942, and it was opened in September 1943 as part of No. 19 Group of the chain of RAF Coastal Command airfields around the British coastline. The original plan for this most westerly airfield was to base a United States Navy anti-submarine unit, equipped with a Consolidated PBY4Y Liberator. However, the USN unit went to Dunkeswell in Devon and RAF Coastal Command took over the airfield instead.

The first RAF unit to occupy the new airfield at St David's was a detachment of Boeing B19 Fortress IIs of Nos 206 and 220 Squadrons from Thorney Island in December 1943. The RAF Fortresses were never quite successful in the role of day bombers, as first emphasised, and a number were transferred to Coastal Command, who had a shortage of long-range land-based aircraft. The detachments remained in Pembrokeshire for a few months on convoy and anti-submarine patrols. The aircraft were able to patrol over 700 miles into the Atlantic.

The first RAF Coastal Command squadron to be based at St David's was No. 517 Met Squadron in November 1943, equipped with eighteen four-engine Handley Page Halifax Met Mk IIIs, plus six spare, and Mk V

A Liberator GRVIII of No. 220 Squadron from St David's.

HP Halifax Met V of No. 517 Squadron operated out of Brawdy gathering important weather information for the Allies.

Another squadron based in Pembrokeshire was No. 58, equipped with Halifaxes.

reconnaissance bombers. Met Mk IIIs and Vs were very similar in many respects. The aircraft were fitted with either Gee or LORAN for navigation; radio altimeters provided the crew with accurate height-keeping on long missions over water as pressure altimeters tended to be inaccurate; a psychrometer was used for measuring temperature and humidity. Several Halifaxes were fitted with ASV Mk2 radar at the maintenance unit at St Athan's.

Halifax GR II Srs I and 1A of Nos 58 and 502 Squadrons followed No. 517 Squadron on 8 and 11 December 1943. From the offset, both squadrons were involved in anti-shipping and anti-submarine duties. On 24 December 1943 (Christmas Eve), eight Halifaxes took off from St David's to attack an enemy convoy in the English Channel. Several enemy ships were sunk and damaged. In January 1944, four U-boats were attacked and depth charged, with two in the same day. During the attacks, Halifaxes dropped five tons of depth charges, disabling two German U-boats despite the terrible weather. During another patrol, one E-boat and a cargo ship were sunk in the Bay of Biscay. In February 1944, a Halifax returning to base after a long patrol in the Bay of Biscay was attacked by a Junkers Ju88s, causing the aircraft to crash into St Brides' Bay with no survivors. Another Halifax was attacked but managed to limp home safely to St David's.

Brawdy, the satellite airfield for St David's, was officially opened on 2 February 1944. It relieved the overcrowding at St David's; No. 517 Met Squadron Halifax was transferred to the new base, where they operated from until November 1945. The site at Brawdy was chosen as it was closest to the Western Approaches and within flying range to the Bay of Biscay. When the squadron moved to Brawdy on 2 February 1944, it was allocated Epicure patrol in the Atlantic and the Bay of Biscay. This involved gathering weather reports and anti-submarine patrols.

The meteorological unit was responsible for gathering weather information over the Atlantic Ocean and the Bay of Biscay, which proved invaluable for the military high command during operational planning. The Met aircraft would fly at different altitudes to gather barometer pressures and temperatures. The data was then analysed by meteorologists in the UK and used to plot approaching weather fronts over the British Isles and Europe. It was units such as this that provided regular, precise forecasts for the D-Day landings.

Despite its function, the squadron was not immune to the problems brought about by bad weather and mechanical faults; losses were mostly attributed to these factors rather than enemy action. On several occasions, aircraft were diverted as far as Gibraltar or bases in North Africa on account of the weather.

Crews of No. 58 Squadron discuss their forthcoming patrol.

The Luftwaffe utilised Focke Wulf Fw200 Condors, anti-shipping aircraft, for weather gathering operations. According to some sources, although denied by the RAF, there was an understanding between the air crews that neither side would interfere with each other in the event of an encounter, but pilots and gun crews were always on alert.

Within days of opening, RAF Brawdy and the surrounding area was attacked by a large force of Junkers Ju88s. Fortunately, the raiders were intercepted and shot down over St Brides' Bay by fighters based at Fairwood Common. A returning Halifax was caught up in the fire-fight and was presumably shot down, as only a single main wheel was ever found. Another Halifax low on fuel managed to dodge the combat area and was able to reach the airfield in safety.

From February 1944, Nos 58 and 502 Squadrons operated from both St David's and Brawdy, as the airfield had become the squadrons' second base. It was during this arrangement that the squadrons recorded several outstanding successes. On 17 March 1944, while on patrol, Flying Officer Galbraith sighted two enemy surface vessels and dropped 2,000 lbs of bombs on the targets. One vessel was left ablaze and by the time another

A Halifax of No. 502 Squadron after a forced landing at Brawdy. (*via RAF Brawdy*)

aircraft returned to the scene, one of the ships had sunk and the crew had abandoned the other. Later, Flying Officer Galbraith was awarded the DFC and the George Medal for his exploits whilst serving No. 502 Squadron based in west Wales. The George Medal was awarded for his airmanship when, having been attacked by seven Ju88s, with one of his air gunners killed and another crew member wounded, he out-flew the enemy aircraft and returned to the base safely. Some of Galbraith's crew were also decorated: Flight Sergeant Forbes, the flight engineer, was awarded the George Medal and DFM, and 1st Lieutenant C. D. Kramer USAAF, on loan to Coastal Command, received the American Medal for Bravery.

On 25 April 1944, Flight Lieutenant Holderness sunk a U-boat during one of his night patrols. This was a classic Coastal Command Halifax night attack; after hours of patient patrol usually without any contact, a blip appeared on the radar screen. Flares were dropped on the contact, illuminating a U-boat. The Halifax dived on the target, dropping its bombs; most missed but one found its target and the submarine was cut in half. The Halifax returned to St David's with only a 37 mm cannon shell hole in its wing.

Back at base at Brawdy, in a small ceremony on 24 May 1944, Squadron Leader C. A. Maton was promoted to commanding officer of No. 502 Squadron with the rank of Wing Commander. It was a landmark occasion in Coastal Command history for a rear gunner to be promoted all the way to squadron CO.

Throughout the next few months the two squadrons were extremely busy; on 3 June, a U-boat was attacked and badly damaged while it was sheltering in Guernsey harbour; on 4 July, four enemy submarines and seven surface targets were attacked and sunk, including a German destroyer on the north-west coast of France. It was during this attack that a Halifax, piloted by Wing Commander Grant, the commanding officer of No. 58 Squadron, was shot down. A Canadian frigate rescued most of the crew but tragically two died from their injuries. Other crews were not so fortunate to be rescued. The crew of Halifax LK962 crashed into the Atlantic on 14 November 1944, with no sign of survivors. The reason for the crash is still unknown but it is believed that it was mechanical failure rather than enemy action.

No. 517 Squadron was classed as a front-line operational squadron, and on a number of occasions it was involved in skirmishes with enemy aircraft. Yet, still, the weather and the chance of a mechanical fault posed a very serious risk. In June 1944, Halifax LL144, code X9 – 'F' for Freddie, piloted by Flying Officer Aveling, a Canadian serving in the RAF, was on a weather gathering mission in connection with the D-Day operations. Some 800 miles from the Pembrokeshire coast and well into the mission, the aircraft developed engine failure. After deciding that there was no hope of returning to Brawdy or any airfield for that matter, Aveling ditched the Halifax in the Atlantic and the crew was able to climb into their dinghies.

A Halifax crew about to embark on a dusk patrol from St David's.

Eventually, after three days adrift, they were picked up by an American ship and taken to the United States.

The crosswinds had always been a concern at St David's and caused several mishaps during take-off and landings. In June 1944, the wind caused Halifax 'F' for Freddie (HX177) to veer off the runway, crashing into the control tower. The aircraft broke in half, but fortunately there were no serious injuries to the crew and the personnel in the tower.

Since the invasion of the Channel Islands, the island ports had been a haven for U-boats sheltering and refuelling, but they also became a graveyard for many. Pembrokeshire-based Halifaxes found the island ports a rich picking area for enemy submarines. During the initial D-Day landings in Normandy, No. 502 Squadron operated from Brawdy a large-scale sweep against U-boats and enemy shipping patrols in the English Channel. At least two U-boat hits were claimed; two of the personnel were awarded the DFC, and nine were mentioned in Despatches in the half yearly honours.

On 8 June 1944, St David's-based Halifax 'F' for Freddie of No. 502 Squadron, captained by Flight Officer J. Spurgeon, took off with a full load of fuel and ordnance on a long patrol. At about 0145, an hour into the patrol, the crew sighted and attacked U-413. The aircraft made its run in on the target with its front .303-inch guns firing. Despite accurate heavy flak coming from the submarine, Spurgeon and his crew managed to drop four 600 lb anti-submarine bombs. Three of the bombs missed the target, but the fourth seriously damaged the conning tower. Sensing a kill, the Halifax made four more machine gun attacks on the submarine; on the

Halifax GRII of No. 502 Squadron flying over the Pembrokeshire countryside.

fifth it received a direct hit on its port engine and had to break off the engagement. Due to substantial damage, the Halifax was unable to return to base, so Flight Officer Spurgeon decided to make for RAF Predannack in Cornwall, where he landed safely. The damaged U-boat limped back to a French port and was out of action for some time.

On 20 June 1944, the Channel Island ports became a target once again when No. 502 Squadron's commanding officer, Wing Commander Morton, led a low level raid on U-boats sheltering in St Peter's port, Guernsey. Following this, on 23 June, Halifax 'T' for Tommy of No. 58 Squadron sunk an enemy submarine in Alderney harbour. In the post D-Day period, both Nos 58 and 502 Squadrons' Halifaxes were reverted back to their bomber role and involved in 'Ranger' patrols over mainland Europe.

As the Allied armies advanced through Europe, RAF Coastal Command reduced the number of their airfields in the UK, especially those specialising in anti-shipping and anti-submarine. The only bases that remained were the flying boat stations and the bases on the south coast of England. With the departure No. 58 Squadron for Stornaway in August 1944, and No. 502 Squadron in September, St David's airfield diminished in importance and Brawdy became the active airfield.

No. 517 Squadron remained at Brawdy until 30 November 1945. After that, all Coastal Command activities from Welsh bases were operated by flying boats based at Pembroke Dock, although various fighter units were always on the look-out for a U-boat periscope or coning tower.

By 1945, most Coastal Command land-based squadrons had converted to the Consolidated Liberator. In 1945, Nos 53 and 220 Squadrons operated from St David's.

CHAPTER 9

Air Defence against the Bomber

German U-boats were the main threat against the sea lanes and coastal shipping around Wales, but a new threat emerged in the Second World War. The enemy bomber not only bombed coastal shipping and military installations, but cities, towns, villages and ports.

When the might of the German war machine overran France in 1940, Wales came within range of German bombers operating out of the French airfields, putting every individual in the country at risk. Six fighter airfields were established in Wales to protect the vital industrial and dockland areas and to provide coastal patrols. Other airfields were utilised for training and storage, with a secondary role as fighter stations. Half of the six fighter bases were in north Wales (Llanbedr, Valley, and Wrexham), and half in the south (Angle, Fairwood Common, and Pembrey). Even before these airfields were built, Carew in Pembrokeshire and Penrhos in Gwynedd provided a minimum fighter cover for their designated areas. As the war progressed, Maintenance Units at Hawarden and St Athan's had their own Fighter Pool or Battle Flights for the base and area defence.

Although the RAF camp at Penrhos was not officially regarded as a fighter station for air defence or for convoy protection sailing the Irish Sea, its squadrons on training exercise were often involved in skirmishes with enemy aircraft. RAF Penrhos was officially opened on 1 February 1937 as No. 5 Armament Training Camp; in pre-war years, various units passed through the camp, training at the nearby gunnery range at Hells Mouth. During the period known as the 'Phoney War', the training school was on a non-war footing. However, during a routine training exercise, the crew of a Harrow bomber belonging to the No. 9 Bombing and Gunnery School spotted a submarine coning tower two miles south of St Tudwal's Island. Regrettably, the nose turret guns were not armed, but details of the sighting were sent to Coastal Command who despatched an Anson to investigate. Unfortunately, by the time it reached the scene there was

Right: It was not shipping that was in danger, but towns and cities. This photograph shows the aftermath of an air raid on Swansea.

Below: Three Hawker Hurricanes of No. 11 Fighter Pool at St Athan's.

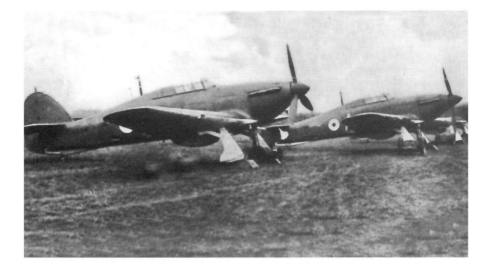

no trace of any vessel. In another incident, an armed Harrow was sent to investigate an Irish steamer acting suspiciously in the Irish Sea. As the result of these sightings, a Fairey Battle was kept in readiness at Penrhos, fully armed with bombs.

Enemy bombers first struck the Llyn Peninsular area on 9 July 1940, when a single German bomber dropped a stick of bombs across Penrhos airfield. The officers' quarters and a hangar were destroyed, and unfortunately two airmen were killed. Before autumn, there were four more attacks on the airfield causing slight damage, but thankfully there were no further casualties. Following these attacks in August 1940, a detachment Spitfire Mk Is of No. 611 Squadron from RAF Ternhill arrived at Penrhos. The squadron provided fighter sweeps of the Irish Sea and over most of north Wales. They were replaced during the winter months by a detachment of Hawker Hurricanes of No. 312 (Czech) Squadron from Speke. The unit was based at Penrhos during perhaps one of the hardest winters for several years. On a number of occasions, the Hurricanes were frozen over and airmen had to chip ice off the wings and fuselage, but it did not deter the squadron from patrolling.

In February 1941, a new airfield with concrete runways was opened at Valley; the detachment left Penrhos to join the rest of the squadron there, where they continued to provide fighter cover for the area.

Whilst fighters were based at Penrhos, no enemy bombers flew near the area. The airfield's air defence had filled an important gap until RAF

No. 312 (Czech) Squadron Hurricanes in a wintry scene at Penrhos. (*via Z. Hurt*)

Valley became operational; with the building of an airfield at Llandwrog, Penrhos' importance diminished even as a training base.

Carew airfield, on the site of the First World War airship station RNAS Pembroke, became operational in the spring of 1939, and was to perform two roles, operational and training, under Coastal Command control.

Due to considerable enemy activity around the south Wales coast, and especially in the vicinity of the steel and coal production areas, the new airfield being built at Pembrey was designated a fighter station to provide air defence for industrial south Wales, the docks of Cardiff, Swansea and the Llanelli area, as well as the coast around south and west Wales. Therefore, having become operational on 1 June 1939 under No. 25 Group, Training Command, for target towing, Pembrey was transferred to Fighter Command, with effect from 20 June 1940.

In 1940, RAF Fighter Command was fully involved in the Battle of Britain. It was a life and death struggle to keep enemy bombers away from the airfields in the Home Counties; very little air defence was offered to the rest of the country. However, it became Fighter Command's policy to give hard-pressed squadrons a rest bite by transferring them to quieter parts of the country to regroup and convert new pilots who had finished their training. As the new Welsh airfields became operational, they were used for this purpose, but the rest periods were usually taken up by scrambles and patrols. While most of the RAF's efforts were concentrated on the south

A line up of Spitfire Mk IIs of No. 350 (Belgian) Squadron at Valley in 1941.

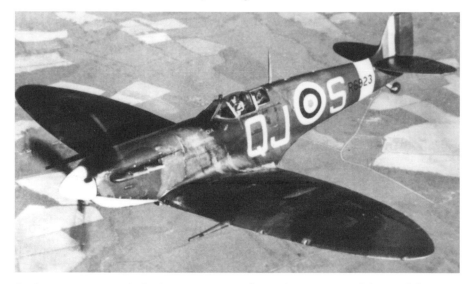

As the war progressed, the Supermarine Spitfire took over most of the air defence in Wales. This photograph shows a Spitfire of No. 92 Squadron in 1940.

of England, especially during the Battle of Britain, several enemy bombers reached the rest of the British Isles, including north and south Wales.

The first fighter squadron to be based at Pembrey in south Wales was No. 92 on 18 June 1940. It came from Hornchurch and was equipped with Supermarine Spitfire Mk IIs under the command of Squadron Leader P. J. Sanders. The squadron was withdrawn from the Battle of Britain for a rest period, but whilst at Pembrey the unit provided convoy patrol around the south Wales coast and beyond.

No. 92 Squadron's first action occurred on 4 July 1940, when a Spitfire of Yellow Section shot down a Ju88 over the Wiltshire countryside. Blue Section, led by the distinguished Flight Lieutenant Robert Stanford Tuck, intercepted a Dornier Do17, but the enemy aircraft escaped into low clouds. Red Section, led by Flight Lieutenant Kingsholme, chased away an enemy bomber which had just bombed a nearby munitions factory. Flight Lieutenant Kingsholme was again in action on 24 July when he shot down a Ju88 over the Bristol Channel.

One pilot that stood out during his stay at Pembrey was Pilot Officer Alan Wright. Flying Spitfire QJ-S on the night of 14/15 August, he helped shoot down a Heinkel He III en-route to bomb Cardiff docks. He had to share the victory with two other famous No. 92 Squadron pilots, Flight Lieutenant R. S. Tuck and Pilot Officer D. G. Williams. Alan Wright was also credited with another Heinkel He III on 29 August and his third on 11 September, while flying out of Biggin Hill.

The majority of bombing was conducted by Heinkel He IIIs and Junker Ju88s. This photograph shows a formation of He IIIs.

German Junkers Ju88 bombers.

Between 28 and 31 August 1940, Hawarden's Battle Flight of three Spitfires were scrambled ten times. On one occasion, Pilot Officer Bratchine, in Spitfire N3235, attacked a Dornier Do215 over the Irish Sea, which crashed in flames off the coast of Anglesey. The Spitfire was also damaged and the pilot had to make a forced landing at Carmel, near Holyhead.

No. 92 Squadron returned to RAF Biggin Hill on 9 September 1940, at the height of the Battle of Britain. The next unit to arrive at Pembrey was No. 79 Squadron on 8 September, with its Hawker Hurricane Mk Is and IIBs, commanded by Squadron Leader J. H. Hayworth. In November, a section of nine Hurricanes engaged a formation of eleven Heinkel He IIIs just off St David's Head, Pembrokeshire, claiming one destroyed and another as probable. Another kill was recorded on 20 November 1940, when a Ju88 was shot down by a Hurricane patrolling near Pembroke Dock flying boat base. The squadron remained at Pembrey until 14 June 1941, when it left for the newly constructed airfield at nearby Fairwood Common on the Gower Peninsula.

In response to the Luftwaffe's night attacks in the south Wales area in the early part of 1941, detachments of Boulton Paul Defiant II night fighters from Nos 256 and 307 Squadrons were based at Pembrey. They remained there from January to March, when No. 256 Squadron departed for Colerne and No. 307 for nearby Fairwood.

The RAF was in urgent need of fighter bases to cover shipping and the industrial areas and ports of the north-west. The Irish Sea and the west

Oil tanks burning at Pembroke Dock. (*PRO*)

coast were as vulnerable as they had been in the First World War. Anglesey was one of the chosen sites for a fighter base in the north as it was in a prominent location, able to cover the Irish Sea and the sea lane along the coast to the Mersey and Liverpool Docks.

RAF Valley is situated on a minor road off the A5 trunk road, near to the small village of Caergeilog and a mile from the village of Valley. The airfield was opened on 1 February 1941 as a Fighter Sector Station under No. 9 Group, which was responsible for protecting the Merseyside area. Its original name was Rhosneiger, but due to pronunciation problems it was changed to Valley on 5 April 1941. The airfield's first commanding officer was Wing Commander J. C. W. Oliver DSO, DFC.

The first unit to be based at Valley was a detachment of Hawker Hurricane Mk Is of No. 312 (Czech) Squadron from RAF Speke, Liverpool, which arrived at Valley on 3 March 1941. At the time, the Czech unit was composed of mainly Battle of Britain veterans who had proved themselves in battle. Within days, the unit was operating standing patrols in the Irish Sea and beyond. The unit remained at Valley until 25 April, when it left for Jurby on the Isle of Man.

On 14 February 1941, No. 316 (Polish, City of Warsaw) Squadron was formed at Pembrey, equipped with Hurricane Mk IIs. The squadron consisted of Polish airmen who had escaped the German onslaught in their country in 1938/39. After some initial problems, eventually resolved by the intervention of the commanding officer of No. 10 Fighter Group, the squadron was declared operational on 25 February. The squadron's first skirmish with the enemy was on 1 April, a few days after the squadron became operational, when a burning ship was spotted off Linney Point being attacked by two Ju88 bombers. In the air battle that followed, the enemy aircraft withdrew, one having sustained serious, most likely fatal, damage.

The squadron's first confirmed kill was on 10 April when an He III preying on coastal shipping was shot down near St Anne's Head, off the coast of Pembrokeshire. By the time the squadron left for Colerne on 16 June 1941, the unit had earned an impressive reputation in a very short time.

On 12 April 1941, No. 79 Squadron was joined at Pembrey by No. 32 Squadron (also equipped with Hurricanes), and both squadrons carried out convoy patrols until they left in June 1941. From February to April 1941, No. 118 Squadron, with Spitfire Mk Is, under the command of Squadron Leader F. J. Howell DFC, arrived at Pembrey for a brief rest period involving convoy patrols and air defence.

Also in April 1941, No. 238 Squadron, flying Hurricane Mk Is & IIs, was stationed at Pembrey, with a detachment of seven aircraft at RAF Carew Cheriton. On 15 April 1941, Carew airfield was attacked by six

Heinkel He III bombers, causing casualties, damaging and destroying several aircraft, and damaging infrastructure. Although the airfield had been bombed three times in 1940, this attack in April 1941 was the most serious. Due to the amount of attention the airfield and surrounding area received from German bombers, a detachment of Hawker Hurricane Mk Is from Nos 32 and 238 Squadrons were despatched from RAF Pembrey in April and May. While the fighters were based at Carew no enemy bomber came near, so the fighters were called upon to provide escorts to Coastal Command aircraft based at the airfield.

The next squadron to arrive at Valley on was No. 615 Squadron on 21 April 1941, equipped with Hurricane Mk IIs from Kenley. The squadron was involved in four combats while on convoy patrols, until it left north Wales on 10 September. An example of a typical sortie undertaken by the squadron occurred on 4 May, when a Junkers Ju88 was damaged off the coast at Holyhead. On 7 May, while Flight Lieutenant Haywood was patrolling at 10,000 feet in his Hurricane over the Menai Straits, he spotted a lone Ju88 some 500 feet above him. As he climbed towards his prey, the enemy bomber escaped into clouds over Snowdonia. On 11 May, GCI station vectored Flight Lieutenant Haywood of No. 615 Squadron towards an enemy aircraft, which he intercepted near Llanberis Pass. After a three second burst, the Hurricane .303-inch guns jammed and the German aircraft managed to escape into the clouds. No. 615 Squadron's next encounter was on 14 May, when Sergeants Hamilton and Roberts

Ground crew of No. 615 Squadron posing in front of a Hurricane at Valley. (*via Squadron Leader Ivor Griffiths*)

engaged a Ju88 10 miles west of Holyhead. Hamilton broke off the engagement when he was hit in the leg by a bullet from the enemy aircraft. Both pilots landed safely at Valley.

Over the next few months, the squadron was involved in several skirmishes with enemy aircraft. Unlike combats, which involved direct and sometimes prolonged air to air fighting, a skirmish could be anything from a single pass on an enemy aircraft, a distant machine gun encounter, or just a chase, usually into clouds.

The newly constructed airfield at Fairwood Common was handed over to the RAF in May 1941, and officially opened within No. 10 Group RAF Fighter Command on 15 July. It was to become the most important fighter base in south Wales. Pembrey was reallocated to Flying Training Command on 15 June 1941 as No. 1 Air Gunnery School, with a relief landing ground at Carew Cheriton in Pembrokeshire.

Angle airfield in Pembrokeshire was declared operational on 1 December 1941 as a forward base in the Fairwood Common Sector under the control of No. 10 Group. Although it had been used by Fighter Command since the summer, the first squadron to be officially based at Angle was No. 32 Squadron, equipped with Hawker Hurricane Mk Is, under the command of Squadron Leader T. Grier DFC. The squadron arrived from Pembrey on 1 June 1941, and remained at Angle until it left for Manston, Kent,

A Bristol Beaufighter belonging to Wing Commander Clerke of No. 125 Squadron at Fairwood.

Personnel of No. 421 (Canadian) Squadron in front of a Spitfire at Angle in November 1942. (*Canadian Archives*)

in November 1941. No. 32 Squadron provided air defence for the south-west sector and St Georges Channel.

To cope with enemy night bombing runs in the north-west, 'A' Flight of No. 219 Squadron from Tangmere, equipped with four Bristol Beaufighter Mk IFs and fitted with AI radar, was posted to Valley on 10 May 1941. The Beaufighter (multi-role fighter) was the most suitable aircraft at the time for the various roles it was required to perform. It was exceptionally suited for convoy patrols as it had a very long range and was a match for any German bombers with its four 20 mm cannons and up to six .303-inch machine guns.

It was No. 219 Squadron that claimed the first kill on 1 June 1941, when a Beaufighter flown by Squadron Leader Colbeck-Welch shot down an enemy aircraft, a crippled Ju88, believed to have been damaged by anti-aircraft fire, some twelve miles off the coast of Aberystwyth.

The first squadron to be stationed at the new Fairwood Common airfield was No. 79 Squadron of Hawker Hurricane Mk Is, transferred from nearby Pembrey on 14 June 1941. While at Fairwood, the squadron had three commanding officers, Wing Commanders G. D. Haysom, G. L. Sinclair, and C. D. Smith. One of the squadron's most famous pilots was Roland Beaumont DFC, who was the flight commander at the time. Until 27 December 1941, the squadron remained at Fairwood where they provided stand-by fighter cover and conversion on to Mk IIBs, ready for

A Bristol Beaufighter about to take off on patrol.

their deployment to India. The unit participated with No. 504 Squadron in a daring daylight raid on Brest on 24 July 1941.

Another of the north Wales airfields involved in air defence was located at Llanbedr on low-lying land between the mountain and the sea at the north end of Cardigan Bay. It was officially opened as a RAF camp on 15 June 1941. Several RAF units wanted control of the airfield, but it was handed over to No. 9 Group, which also controlled Valley. The first unit to be based at the airfield, however, was the Elementary Flying Training School, operated by the civilian company Airworks Ltd., with DH Tiger Moths, most of which were requisitioned civilian aircraft.

Bristol Beaufighter IIs of No. 600 (City of London) Squadron, a night fighter unit, arrived at Fairwood in south Wales on 17 June 1941 and left on 27 June. They were replaced by Hurricane Mk Is of No. 317 (Polish) Squadron from Colerne. Their stay was also short lived, but the squadron made a name for itself by shooting down a Ju88 some ten miles south of the airfield.

On 28 June, No. 219 Squadron at Valley was joined by another Beaufighter detachment from No. 68 Squadron, based at RAF High Ercall. Two days later, No. 456 RAAF Squadron was formed at Valley, initially equipped with Defiant Mk Is. They later re-equipped with Beaufighter IIF and VIFs. This night fighter squadron had one of the longest associations with the airfield, as it remained at Valley until 30 March 1943.

The other wartime airfield in north Wales was RAF Wrexham, located on a plateau on the outskirts of the town in an area known as Borras. RAF Wrexham was officially opened in June 1941, and initially was intended to house a fighter squadron, hence the concrete runways, as Wrexham

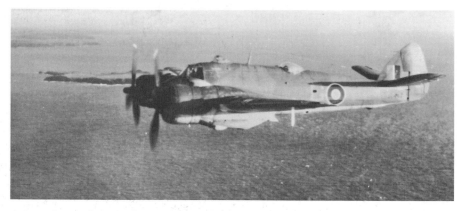

A Bristol Beaufighter of No. 248 Squadron patrolling the Pembrokeshire coastline.

A Hawker Hurricane Mk II of No. 615 Squadron.

The Bristol Beaufighter could be classed as the first multi-task aircraft. In the role of a night fighter, it did valuable work with No. 125 Squadron at Fairwood and Valley. This photograph shows pilots returning from a sortie at RAF Fairwood. (*via Swansea Airport*)

was in the direct path of an enemy bombing route against the north-west industrial areas. However, the first unit to be based at the station was No. 9 Group, Anti Aircraft Co-operation, lightly equipped with Blenheims and Lysanders, which arrived from Speke, Liverpool, on 10 August 1941.

On 11 July, No. 615 Squadron, based at Valley, suffered its first tragedy when a Hurricane flown by Pilot Officer Stepler suffered an engine failure and crash landed on Nefyn Sands. Initially, it was a text book landing, but the aircraft hit a rock and somersaulted, landing upside down in the wet sand. Unfortunately, the pilot was pushed into the wet sand by the weight of the aircraft and was drowned.

No. 615 Squadron's first confirmed kill was on 26 August 1941, when two Hurricanes, flown by Flying Officer Mouchotte and Sergeant Hamilton of 'B' Flight, intercepted a Ju88 over Cardigan Bay. After a brief skirmish, the bomber left the scene with both engines on fire, causing it to crash land in Eire.

In September 1941, No. 125 Squadron, commanded by Wing Commander H. M. Mitchell DFC, arrived at Fairwood, equipped with Boulton Paul Defiant night fighters. The unit specialised in night flying and formed part of the night defences for the industrial and manufacturing areas along the south Wales coast. The Defiant was designed as a two-seat interceptor with armament concentrated in a powered dorsal turret with four .303-inch machine guns. The night fighter version with AI radar eventually equipped eleven squadrons, until it was replaced by Bristol Beaufighter Mk IFs. The squadron moved to RAF Colerne in January 1942, but a detachment remained at Fairwood.

The first front line operational squadron to arrive at Llanbedr was No. 74 Squadron with its Spitfire Mk IIs on 4 October 1941, commanded by Squadron Leader R. G. H. Matthews DFC. The squadron was involved in convoy patrols over the Irish Sea and the occasional scramble.

The first fighter unit to move to RAF Wrexham was No. 96 Squadron from RAF Carnage, which often got waterlogged during the winter months. It took the squadron some months before fully completing the move, but by 21 October 1941 the unit's fourteen Defiant Mk Is and two Hurricane Mk IIs were set up at Wrexham. In the meantime, RAF Fairwood's airfield became a full sector station on October 25.

A typical No. 68 Squadron night fighter patrol operating out of RAF Valley took place on the night of 11/12 October 1941. A Bristol Beaufighter, crewed by Pilot Officer Mansfield and radar operator Sergeant Janacek, were directed by GCI at 10 p.m. towards an enemy aircraft flying over the Irish Sea. At a range of 300 feet, the Beaufighter made a two-second burst of its 20 mm cannons. The Ju88 port engine burst into flames and the aircraft dived into some clouds.

In the early part of the war, the main night fighter was the Boulton Paul Defiant. Crews of No. 96 Squadron based at Wrexham discuss tactics.

Another contact was made at 11 p.m.; Pilot Officer Mansfield observed several hits on the Ju88's wing and fuselage. Once again, the enemy aircraft broke off the engagement. A third contact was made at 11.25 p.m. at a height of 12,000 feet when a lone Ju88 was spotted silhouetted against the moon. After a short burst, the Ju88 starboard wing and engine caught fire; the aircraft soon went out of control and dropped into the clouds, eventually crashing into the sea. Five minutes later, while returning to Valley, Pilot Officer Mansfield spotted another Ju88 which was shot down in the Skerries area. The Beaufighter landed at Valley with only twenty rounds of cannon shells left.

Over the next few months the Beaufighters, in conjunction with GCI station, intercepted several enemy aircraft; a Ju88 was shot down in the sea off Nefyn, and a Heinkel He III was shot down some six miles from Valley, near Gwalchmai.

The Australian No. 456 Squadron became fully operational on 5 September 1941, and operational with Beaufighters on 25 November, therefore relieving No. 68 Squadron from further night interception duties in the area. Due to bad weather, no contact with the enemy was made during December.

On 26 November, a pair of Spitfires belonging to No. 74 Squadron from Llanbedr encountered three Junkers Ju88s; one enemy aircraft was shot down, but unfortunately Pilot Officer Williams was also shot down and killed. The squadron left Llanbedr in January 1942, for Long Kesh in Northern Ireland.

At RAF Valley, No. 456 Squadron's first kill flying Beaufighters was on the night of 10/11 January 1942, when all of No. 9 Group airfields were shut because of bad weather, except Valley. The Luftwaffe had taken advantage of the bad weather and was out in force over Merseyside and the surrounding area. A Beaufighter flown by the Squadron Commander, Squadron Leader J. Hamilton, with Pilot Officer D. L. Norris-Smith as observer, intercepted a mine laying Dornier Do217 at about 12,000 feet after a chase across Wales, and despatched it with two bursts of cannon fire. However, enemy activity in the early part of 1942 was rather infrequent in north Wales.

The first Supermarine Spitfire unit to be based at Angle was No. 312 (Czech) Squadron, which arrived in early February 1942. This unit, after a non-operational spell, was sent to Pembrokeshire to provide convoy patrols and air defence of Milford Haven and its important installations. While at Angle, the squadron flew 231 operational hours and was involved in several skirmishes with enemy aircraft. One such encounter occurred on 16 February, when several Spitfires went to the aid of a Coastal Command

The Hawker Hurricane served with several squadrons protecting the Welsh nation. This photograph shows a Hurricane of No. 312 Squadron at Penrhos. (*via Z. Hurt*)

aircraft under attack. After the brief skirmish, the Spitfires shot down a Junkers Ju88. While at Angle, the squadron's Spitfires were fitted with bomb racks and took part in several ground attack exercises with the army. No. 312 Squadron were also involved in the Ramrod and Rhubarb operations. The squadron's commanding officer at Angle was the Battle of Britain veteran, Squadron Leader H. Bird-Wilson DFC. No. 312 Squadron left Pembrokeshire in April 1942 for its new base at Fairwood Common.

The next squadron to arrive at Llanbedr was No. 131 from Atcham, equipped with Spitfire IIB & VBs, in February 1942. The squadron left for Valley on 10 March 1942, but due to problems with soft sand blowing in off the sand dunes at Valley, several aircraft remained at Llanbedr. It was here that the squadron claimed its first aerial victory when Flight Lieutenant Ray Harries, a Welsh flight commander, shared in the destruction of a Ju88 which crashed 35 miles from the airfield. Ray Harries became the top Welsh pilot with twenty victories. Because of the sand problems at Valley, the squadron returned to Llanbedr in April 1942, and finally left for Merston in May.

In May 1942, Spitfires of No. 232 Squadron were based at Llanbedr for three months. While based at the airfield, the squadron was despatched to Merston to take part in the ill-fated Dieppe Raid. The squadron left Llanbedr in August for Turnhouse airfield in Scotland, to help protect Edinburgh and the Firth of Forth.

Between March 1943 and March 1944, Llanbedr became a temporary home for two Polish squadrons, Nos 302 and 306. No. 312 (Czech) Squadron came to Llanbedr for two weeks in December 1943, and No. 340 (Free French) Squadron came in May 1944.

On 10 March, No. 131 (County of Kent) Squadron, equipped with Spitfire Mk VBs, moved to Valley from RAF Llanbedr for daylight convoy escort duties. Two days later, two Spitfires flown by Flight Lieutenant Harries and Sergeant Vilboux intercepted a Ju88 which had been observed flying at about fifty feet some thirty miles from Holyhead, trying to avoid radar. The two Spitfires dived, firing their guns on the unsuspecting enemy and hitting the port engine which burst into flames; the Ju88 went into a stall and crashed into the sea.

The next unit to be based at Angle was No. 263 Squadron under the command of Squadron Leader R. S. Woodward DFC, and equipped with twin-engine Westland Whirlwind FIs. The single seat twin-engine Westland Whirlwind was designed in 1936 under the direction of W. E. W. 'Teddy' Petter. The prototype first flew on 11 October 1938, and the first production Whirlwind Mk I flew in June 1940. Service introduction began with No. 263 Squadron in July 1940. The Whirlwind was powered by two 860 hp Rolls Royce Peregrine engines, which gave it maximum speed of

360 mph and a range of 800 miles. Only 114 of the type were built, and they served with just two squadrons.

The Whirlwind was an attractive aircraft, but it never achieved its potential as a fighter. However, due to the sheer determination and bravery of its pilots, the aircraft did some very useful work as a bomber. Armed with four Hispano 20 mm cannons in the nose, the Whirlwind should have been an ideal platform for both air to air fighting and ground attack, but it was constantly out manoeuvred by enemy aircraft and therefore suffered heavily. Throughout its brief service life, the Whirlwind was also dogged by both engine and cannon problems. Although most of these problems had been ironed out by the time No. 263 Squadron arrived at Angle, the Whirlwind still caused considerable headaches for the ground crews. To compound matters, during the squadron's move to Angle, a railway truck carrying the aircraft's 20 mm cannon shells caught fire just outside Llanelli railway station, causing in a spectacular explosion and considerable damage to nearby buildings. Despite these problems, No. 263 Squadron continued to provide convoy protection in the Irish Sea and took part in bombing raids on the continent.

While No. 263 Squadron was based at Angle, a detachment of ten Whirlwinds was sent to Portreath in Cornwall to take part in the first Ramrod operations over France. The first raid took place on 30 April 1942, when Whirlwinds escorted by Spitfires of No. 310 Squadron attacked

In 1942, No. 263 Squadron, equipped with twin-engine Westland Whirlwind F1s, were based at Angle for coastal protection. (*T. Rennie*)

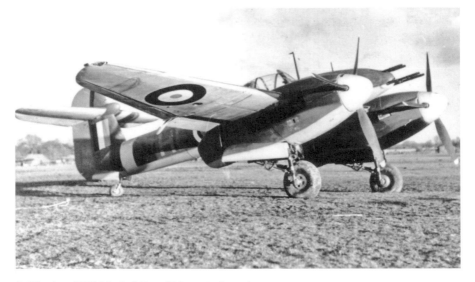

A Westland Whirlwind F1 of No. 263 Squadron.

enemy airfields of Lannion and Morlaix. Several enemy aircraft, mostly Heinkel He III and Junkers Ju88s, were destroyed or damaged, as well as several airfield installations. All RAF aircraft returned safely. Further raids were repeated on 5 June, causing further destruction to enemy airfields.

During the Baedecker raids by the Luftwaffe on Bath on the nights of 26 and 27 April 1942, No. 125 Squadron's Beaufighters, Defiants and Hurricanes from Fairwood and Charmy Down, flew several patrols over the city. During one of the two skirmishes, one enemy aircraft was claimed as probably destroyed and another one damaged. On another occasion, a No. 125 Squadron Beaufighter shot down a Ju88 off the Pembrokeshire coast.

During May 1942, whilst at Wrexham, No. 96 Squadron was re-equipped with Beaufighter Mk IIs, with conversion training done on three twin-engine Airspeed Oxfords borrowed from a neighbouring unit. The squadron retained the Defiant until July, while the conversation took place. The Beaufighter conversion was only marred by one accident, a good record, when aircraft T3414 failed to get airborne during a training exercise, left the runway, and ran across a public road, coming to rest in a small pond. The aircraft was totally destroyed by fire, but due to the sturdy construction of the aircraft, the crew managed to scramble out in time. Also in 1942, No. 285 Squadron became a lodger unit at the airfield and remained there until 29 October 1942.

During his visit to the area on 5 May 1942, the Duke of Kent made a special visit to RAF Wrexham and inspected both Nos 96 and 285 Squadrons. No. 96 Squadron's first Beaufighter patrol took place on 30

June 1942, during the King and Queen's royal visit to a nearby airfield at High Ercall on 16 July 1942. The squadron's Beaufighters kept a standing patrol over Wrexham and the area for approximately four hours.

No. 125 Squadron returned to Fairwood in May 1942 with Bristol Beaufighter IIFs, with a detachment based at Sumburgh and Peterhead in Scotland, and remained in south Wales until April 1943.

The next encounter of No. 456 Squadron, based at Valley, was on the night of 17/18 May. Pilot Officer Wills and his observer Sergeant Lowther were on convoy escort in their Beaufighter Mk IIF, flying over St George's Channel. They sighted a German Ju88 shadowing the convoy; after playing hide and seek in and out of clouds, Pilot Officer Wills caught glimpse of the aircraft and opened up with their 20 mm cannon. The first burst was at 350 yards, the second at 250 yards, and the final burst was at 200 yards, at which point the Junkers slipped into thick cloud cover. A week later it was reported that the Ju88 had crashed into the sea five miles from Bardsey Island.

No. 263 Squadron's first casualty since moving to Angle was when Me109s shot down two Whirlwinds over France during a Rhubarb raid on 23 July. Unfortunately, both pilots were killed.

On 30 July, Wing Commander Wolfe and Pilot Officer Ashcroft of No. 456 Squadron intercepted a Heinkel He III whilst on patrol over Llyn Peninsular. The He III crashed in flames on Pwllheli beach. The squadron's Beaufighters remained vigilant at all times, and for the next few months were regularly vectored to radar contacts.

During November, No. 456 Squadron began patrolling further to the south towards Milford Haven, and as far as the Scilly Isles. This helped to relieve the pressure on aircraft based in Pembrokeshire. For the rest of the year the squadron provided escorts to incoming USAAF aircraft.

In August 1942, No. 263 Squadron left Angle for RAF Colerne, and was replaced by No. 152 Squadron Spitfires. This squadron's stay in Angle was short; within weeks it was re-posted to RAF Wittering to be re-equipped with Spitfire VBs. On 23 August, while based at Angle, two Spitfires on patrol shot down a Ju88, but, unfortunately, on another patrol, two of the squadron's aircraft collided in bad weather.

As the number of air raids in the north-west diminished, the importance of RAF Wrexham as a fighter base also diminished; the airfield was transferred to Flying Training Command as a satellite airfield to nearby Carnage.

No. 96 Squadron left RAF Wrexham on 6 September 1942 for Honiley, to provide the defence of the midlands against night attacks. To enhance night fighting ability in the south Wales sector, No. 536 (Turbinlite) Squadron arrived at Fairwood in early October 1942. The squadron was equipped with Douglas Havoc Mk IIs and fitted with a searchlight for night fighting. The concept was that the Havoc would light up an enemy aircraft whilst a Hurricane, flying with the Havoc, would shoot it down. The concept was unsuccessful insomuch as it was overtaken by the AI radar, fitted to the Beaufighter and Mosquito aircraft. The squadron was therefore disbanded at Fairwood on 25 January 1943.

From November 1942 to January 1943, No. 421 (RCAF) Squadron, with its Spitfire VBs, under the command of Squadron Leader F. E. Green DFC, became the resident fighter unit at RAF Angle. The squadron's Spitfires provided fighter cover for the area and for the Irish Sea convoys, but made little contact with the enemy. Unfortunately, the squadron lost two aircraft in a collision near the airfield. One Spitfire crashed in the sea near Thorne Point and the pilot was able to swim ashore, while the other aircraft crashed on the airfield killing the pilot.

In January 1943, No. 456 Squadron began converting to the De Havilland Mosquito NF II, which became the squadron's standard aircraft for the rest of the war. The squadron left Valley on 29 March 1943, and was replaced by No. 406 (Canadian) Squadron, equipped with Beaufighter Mk VIs. Most of the squadron's work was in escorting American aircraft. The squadron remained at Valley until October, when it was replaced by another night fighting unit, No. 125 Squadron.

In January 1943, another Canadian unit, No. 412 Squadron, equipped with Spitfires, arrived at Angle under the command of Squadron Leader F. W. Kelly. Their stay was only temporary as the squadron moved to Fairwood in February. All these short stays caused great problems to the

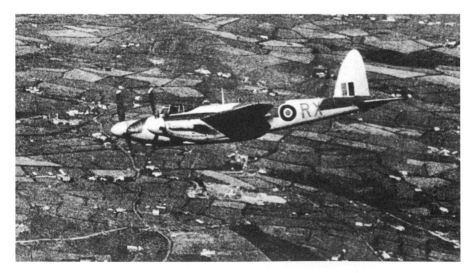

A De Havilland Mosquito NF VI of No. 456 (Australian) Squadron.

A Supermarine Spitfire Mk V of No. 402 (Canadian) Squadron.

base and especially to the squadrons. On several occasions, by the time ground crews arrived at Angle, their squadron had already moved on to another base, causing a shortage in man power. For the next few months there was a lull in squadron movements, which gave the airfield personnel a breather.

Squadrons based at Fairwood remained vigilant throughout, and were often scrambled to intercept night intruders. On 16 February 1943, No. 125 Squadron's Beaufighters were scrambled against a flight of Dornier Do217s that had attacked the airfield, killing three airwomen and causing some damage. The pursuing Beaufighters shot down two of the raiders; one German aircraft was cut in two by the overwhelming firepower of the Beaufighter's four 20 mm cannons and six .303-inch machine guns.

That night, Pilot Officer H. Newton was credited with the destruction of both German aircraft, the second of which he shared with Flight Lieutenant W. Jameson. On his return to base, Jameson's radar operator, Pilot Officer Crookes, was shot in the leg (by a .303-inch calibre round) and an unexploded 20 mm cannon shell was embedded in the Beaufighter's fuselage. Pilot Officer Newton was awarded the DFC for his actions.

Also that night, another raider, a Dornier Do217 from 5th Staffel, KG2, was shot down by Wing Commander R. F. H. Clerke, commanding officer of No. 125 Squadron, with Pilot Officer D. H. Spurgeon as his radar operator.

On 15 April 1943, No. 307 (Polish) Squadron, equipped with De Havilland Mosquitoes Mk IIs, arrived at Fairwood for long-range convoy escort and Ranger sweeps over the continent. On 4 June, during their stay at Fairwood, the Duke of Gloucester made an inspection of the base, personally talking to each member of the squadron.

Towards the end of June 1943, Fairwood's status as an active operational airfield ceased. It became a training station for Fighter Command, still under No. 10 Group, although a night fighting unit remained at the base.

The RAF Fighter Sector closed on 1 November 1943 and all operations moved to Woodvale, leaving Nos 275 (ASR) and 125 Squadrons for air defence and the protection of incoming American aircraft. As well as providing air defence, the resident RAF squadrons at Valley were also used to acting as shepherds to incoming American aircraft that were lost or in trouble, which happened quite often.

The resident squadron at Valley from November 1943 was No. 125, equipped with Beaufighter VIFs. The squadron's first call was on 18 November 1943, when two Beaufighters were scrambled to go to the assistance of a crippled Liberator which had been attacked by a Ju88 over the Bay of Biscay. Unfortunately, the enemy bomber had disappeared by the time the Beaufighters arrived, but the Liberator, escorted by No. 125 aircraft, limped back to Valley and landed safely.

In December, aircraft from Valley had to search for a flight of incoming USAAF B17s, which were lost, flying in circles around Cardigan Bay.

A De Havilland Mosquito of No. 264 Squadron at Fairwood in 1943.

Eventually, the flight was found and escorted to the airfield. On 19 December, a total of thirty-eight aircraft managed to reach the airfield safely, some escorted by the Beaufighters, a typical example of the various aircraft that found shelter at Valley.

While at Valley, No. 125 Squadron was re-equipped with the more agile multi-role aircraft, the Rolls Royce Merlin powered DH Mosquito XVI in early 1944. The squadron left for Hurn, Bournemouth, on 24 March 1944. By the middle of 1944 nearly all enemy air activity had ceased in the north Wales area.

For three weeks in March 1944, No. 485 (New Zealand) Squadron, commanded by Squadron Leader J. B. Niven, became RAF Llanbedr's resident defence squadron. Equipped with Supermarine Spitfires, the squadron patrolled the Irish Sea and as far north as Belfast and the Isle of Man. On a number of occasions, its fighters were vectored to a contact picked up by radar, but most of the contacts were either lone Allied aircraft on training flights or a USAAF aircraft which had lost its bearings.

In March 1944, No. 68 Squadron, equipped with twenty-five Bristol Beaufighter VIFs under the command of Wing Commander D. Haley Bell DFC, arrived at Fairwood to provide night fighter cover. Fairwood night fighters were also responsible for most of the south-western part of England, and patrols around the Exeter area became a standard pattern. During one patrol on 27 March 1944, two Beaufighters of No. 68 Squadron were diverted on to enemy aircraft. One Ju88 was shot down near Wells, and the rest limped home with cannon shell holes in their fuselage. By the summer of 1944, the threat of enemy bombers had diminished, and, in June, No. 68 Squadron Beaufighters moved to Castle Camp in Cambridge.

Fighter squadrons rotated through Fairwood's two Armament Practice Camps at a very fast pace. In most cases their stays were only for few weeks or even less; the courses would last from ten days to two weeks. However, during their stay at Fairwood, the squadron's secondary role was to carry out convoy patrols around the Welsh coast, as well as air defence of the important installations and cities. Fairwood was often used as a rest base for some of the front line squadrons, as well as a base for squadron conversion and re-equipping towards the end of the war.

From March to April 1944, No. 129 Squadron, with its Spitfire IXs and commanded by Squadron Leader C. How DFM, Order of Lenin (one of the few foreigners to win such decoration), arrived at Llanbedr from Heston. Spitfire squadrons were usually sent to Llanbedr for a rest period, but they still shared the responsibility for air defence of the north-west and patrolling the Irish Sea. Numerous squadrons just stayed for a brief period ranging from a few hours to a few days, which caused great strain on the ground crews at the base.

It was not only the RAF that used Llanbedr airfield. On a number of occasions, USAAF Thunderbolts, P51 Mustangs, and P38 Lightnings shared the facilities with the RAF.

By the summer of 1944, enemy activities over the north-west and the Irish Sea had diminished, and therefore Llanbedr was not required as a fighter base. Llanbedr had always played an important part as a gunnery-training base and was reverted to this role. Air defence was only allocated to two airfields in Wales, one in the north at Valley, and one in south Wales at Fairwood Common.

To cope with the an increase in aerial operations over the Irish Sea and the Bristol Channel, Air Sea Rescue Squadrons were based at Fairwood Common (No. 275) and at RAF Valley (No. 276). The RAF Mountain Rescue unit also deserves a mention. They were volunteers who risked life and limb to save downed airmen in the mountains of north Wales. The unit was formed at RAF Llandwrog, but moved to Llanbedr in 1945.

In the First World War, shipping lanes around Wales were the main targets for enemy U-boats, but twenty-one years later ordinary people working in factories, in the ports, or just living in towns and cities were also targeted.

Airmen of the Royal Air Force and the Fleet Air Arm became national heroes for their desperate fight to keep the Welsh skies free of enemy aircraft. A great debt is also owed to all the services: the Royal Navy for their tireless patrols and escort duties; the Army for manning the coastal defences; and the Merchant Navy, whose determined efforts and sacrifice provided the nation with food and raw materials for the war effort.

Finally, praise is due to the people of Wales, who, like the rest of the British, put up with rationing, bombing, and the loss of their possessions, but kept their spirits up nonetheless.

CHAPTER 10

Airfields and Bases

The location of Wales on the western side of Great Britain, near to the Western Approaches and the west coast shipping lanes, made it inevitable that certain places within the country would be chosen as sites for airfields and military bases in wartime. During the First and Second World Wars, a total of thirty-seven airfields and four relief landing grounds were built in Wales, eleven of which were operationally involved in air defence and maritime operations.

In the First World War, there were four bases directly involved in anti-submarine duties, keeping the sea lanes open and free from enemy interference. In the Second World War there were two main fighter stations (Fairwood Common and Valley) and a number of subsidiaries (e.g. Angle, Llanbedr, Pembrey and Wrexham). Most of the airfields in Pembrokeshire were under the control of RAF Coastal Command and played a significant part in the Battle of the Atlantic. The rest of the airfields built were used for training and various support roles.

Locations of First World War Airfields and Bases.

Bangor(Aber), Gwynedd.

The landing site was situated in the coastal area between Bangor and the village of Abergwyngregin. Fifty acres of land, consisting of most of Glan y Mor Isaf farm, was requisitioned in May 1918. The landing ground at the airship station at RNAS Anglesey, Llangefni, was found unsuitable for aircraft operations and a new site was urgently required.

Several hedges were removed to give the field a run of about 1,000 feet. Four Bessoneau hangars were erected to house and maintain the aircraft. All accommodation, officers and other ranks were housed in tents and

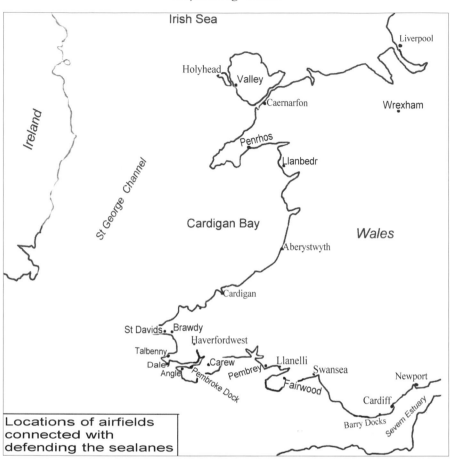

Map of the Welsh airfields and bases.

farm out-buildings. Stores, fuel and ammunition were kept in nearby woods, away from the main site, protected by sand bags and covered by tarpaulins. No. 530 Special Duties Flight, equipped with Airco DH-6 aircraft, was formed at Bangor in August 1918 as part of No. 244 Squadron. The squadron was disbanded on 22 January 1919, and soon afterwards the landing ground was dismantled and the site returned to its previous owners.

Fishguard, Pembrokeshire.

The RNAS seaplane station was located on the sea shore close to the northern breakwater of the port of Goodwick. It had a single slipway and launching crane on the break water, three adjoining wooden buildings

Aerial photo of RAF Hayscastle Cross. Note the shadows of the radar masts. (*Welsh Assembly Archives*)

Aerial photograph of Penrhos airfield in Gwynedd. (*Welsh Assembly Archives*)

to house the seaplanes, and one Bessoneau hangar. Further buildings, including accommodation, a wireless room, a guard room, a women's rest room, a photographic hut and workshops, were added later. The officers were billeted in nearby Fishguard Bay Hotel. The base was officially classed as operational in March 1917, and the first seaplane was delivered to the unit on 13 April 1917.

There were two naval seaplane flights stationed at Fishguard, equipped with Sopwith Baby, Fairey Hamble Baby and Short Type 184s. The two flights became No. 245 Squadron on 20 August 1918, standardizing on one type, the Short 184. The squadron was disbanded on 10 May 1919, by which time it had been reduced to a few aircraft. Soon afterwards, the station was closed and most of the infrastructure was dismantled and removed.

Llangefni (RNAS Anglesey).

RNAS Anglesey, located between the A5 and the B5109 roads, was fortunate to have an all round clearance. Several places in Anglesey were considered as sites for airship operations, but the Admiralty eventually acquired over 200 acres of farm land 3 miles from the town of Llangefni. The air station consisted of a large 120 x 318 feet airship shed, with large windshields on either end. Several wooden and corrugated iron huts were constructed as workshops, stores, and for gas production units. Accommodation and a Bessoneau hangar were added later near the main road.

Aerial photograph of RNAS Anglesey (Llangefni).

RNAS Anglesey was a base for Sea Scout SS Type, Sea Scout Pusher SSP Type, and Sea Scout Zero Type SSZ airships. On 6 June 1918, No. 521 (A Flight) and No. 522 (B Flight) Coastal Patrol Flights were formed at Llangefni, equipped with eight Airco DH-4s. The Flights were part of No. 255 Squadron RNAS until 15 August, when the unit moved to the new base at Aber (Bangor), where it was renumbered No. 244 Squadron.

The Llangefni site was ideal for airships, but the ground was rather uneven for aircraft operations. The station closed in 1919, but the Admiralty did not relinquish the site until 1920.

Milton (RNAS Pembroke).

The base at Milton occupied some 228 acres near the village of Sageston, just off the main road between Pembroke and Carmarthen. The airship station consisted of two 112 x 338 feet corrugated iron hangars with windshields, two lots of hydrogen storage tanks constructed next to the hangars, and the gas production units. Wooden and canvas workshops were also built. Accommodation consisted of a mixture of wooden and canvas huts. Bessoneau hangars were later built for the naval aircraft stationed on the base.

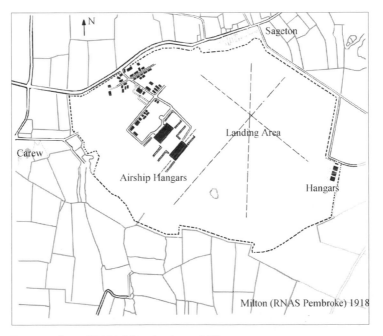

Layout plan of RNAS Pembroke at Milton.

Aerial photograph of RNAS Pembroke. (*B. Turpin via D. Brock*)

The site operated the Sea Scout SS type, the large Coastal class, and the Sea Scout Zero SSZ type, which were actively involved in patrolling the sea lanes and the Western Approaches. On 29 April 1917, the airships were joined by aircraft of the Navy's Special Patrol Flight, equipped with Sopwith 1½ Strutter bombers, and later joined by Airco DH-4s. The flight was part of No. 255 Squadron which covered all of Wales. In 1918, Flight Nos 519 and 520 joined to become No. 244 Squadron. Fishguard and RNAS Pembroke came under the command of No. 14 Group, with its headquarters in Haverfordwest. No. 244 Squadron was disbanded during February and March 1919.

In 1920, the Admiralty relinquished the site and it was eventually demolished. Some ten years later, the site was chosen for an airfield with concrete runways.

Locations of Second World War Airfields and Bases.

Angle, Pembrokeshire.

RAF Angle was planned and built in 1940, and was declared operational in May 1941. It was located just off the B4320 road, which connects the

Aerial Photograph of
Angle. (*Welsh Assembly
Archives*)

village of Angle and the castle town of Pembroke. The first squadron to
use the airfield was No. 32 Squadron of Hawker Hurricanes in early June
1941. It was not until 1 December that Angle became a forward base in
the Fairwood Common sector under No. 10 Group, Fighter Command,
whose responsibility was to provide fighter cover for south Wales and the
south-west of England. The airfield had three surfaced runways, the longest
being 4,800 feet long, with one T2 hangar, four Blister-type hangars, and a
number of dispersal points.

Between 1941 and July 1943, several fighter squadrons operated from the
airfield on convoy patrols and air defence in south Wales. As enemy aircraft
activities diminished, so too did RAF Angle's importance as a fighter base;
the airfield was temporarily handed over to the Fleet Air Arm. In September,
it was again transferred back to the RAF and used for training.

RAF Angle officially closed on 1 January 1946. One event that made
Angle famous was Flight Officer Gordon Singleton's emergency landing at
the airfield in a Short Sunderland on 29 May 1943, whilst he was operating
out of Pembroke Dock.

Brawdy, Pembrokeshire.

Brawdy airfield, situated just off the A478 Haverfordwest to St David's road, became operational on 2 February 1944, under the control of RAF Coastal Command. It was originally intended as a satellite to nearby St David's, but on 1 November 1945, station headquarters and its squadrons were officially transferred from St David's to Brawdy, leaving the former to become the satellite airfield.

Brawdy had three runways, two of which awere 6,000 feet in length, capable of operating the heaviest Coastal Command aircraft. There were twenty-seven spectacle type dispersal points. During the Second World War, the airfield had three T2 hangars for maintenance and storage. In 1944, there were eighty-two officers based at the airfield, including I WAAF, and 1,321 other ranks, of which 185 were WAAF. The main squadron based at Brawdy was No. 517 Meteorological Squadron, equipped with Handley Page Halifaxes. In January 1946, the airfield was handed over to Admiralty control.

Carew Cheriton, Pembrokeshire.

Carew airfield was located on the site of the First World War airship station, RNAS Pembroke. It is situated just off the A477, Pembroke Dock to St Clear's road. Construction took place during the summer of 1938,

Photograph of Carew airfield, taken in 1944. (*via D. Brock*)

A Lockheed Hudson.

and the airfield was opened a year later. Carew's role was to support the flying boat station at Pembroke Dock, but during the Second World War it had two roles: operational and training under No. 15 Group, Coastal Command.

Carew consisted of three concrete runways, with the main site located on either side of the A477 road. At the outbreak of war, several detachments were attached to the airfield for coastal patrols, including Nos 48 and 217 Squadrons, equipped with Avro Ansons. A Coastal Patrol Flight was also formed at the airfield.

While the other airfields were being built in the county, Carew hosted a number of fighter units for air defence and escort for the patrol aircraft. In 1940–44, the airfield became the base for Dutch personnel who had escaped from occupied Holland with their Fokker T-VIIIs. These were replaced by Ansons and later Lockheed Hudsons. The airfield was transferred to Flying Training Command on 24 July 1942, and to Technical Training Command on 5 October. The station was officially closed on 24 November 1945.

Dale, Pembrokeshire.

Dale airfield was located on the northern side of Milford Haven, near the village of Dale and Marloes. It was built in 1941 as a satellite to Talbenny airfield to the north. It had three concrete and tarmac runways, 3,495 feet, 4,215 feet and 4,785 feet in length. Dispersal points, hangars, workshops, and most of the accommodation blocks were to the north-west of the runways, with the main entrance towards Marloes. The airfield became fully operational on 1 June 1942 under the control of No. 19 Group, RAF Coastal Command.

The first squadron to be based at the airfield was No. 304 (Polish) Squadron, equipped with Vickers Wellington ICs (one of the bomber units transferred to Coastal Command). The aircraft flew maritime reconnaissance patrols until they left in March 1943.

In September 1943, the Admiralty exchanged its base at Angle for Dale, which it regarded as better suited for Fleet Air Arm operations. It remained under Admiralty control until it closed on 13 December 1947.

Fairwood Common, Glamorganshire.

Fairwood Common was opened for No. 10 Group, RAF Fighter Command, on 15 July 1941, and became a full sector station on 25 October. The airfield was situated on the Gower Peninsula, just off the A4118 Swansea to Port Eynon road and some five miles from Swansea. It was built on a flat piece of land known as Fairwood Common.

The airfield had three main runways: one running north-east–south-west and measuring 4,800 feet in length, one running west–east and measuring 4,100 feet, and another of the same length running north-west–south-east. All three runways were interconnected by a unique system of taxiways. Three Bellman and eight Blister type hangars were built at the airfield during the war. In all, there were forty-four aircraft pens and hard standing pens around the airfield.

The first fighter squadron to be based at Fairwood was No. 79, equipped with Hawker Hurricane Mk Is. Over the next few years, the airfield became a home for numerous fighter squadrons involved in both day and night defence. One squadron that made a name for itself was No. 125, equipped with Defiants and, later, Beaufighters. Also based at Fairwood were two armament practice units, primarily used by fighter bomber units of Group Nos 83 and 84 and the 2nd Tactical Air Force. Most of the squadrons attending courses at Fairwood had a secondary role of providing air defence for the sector. When the APC was disbanded in May 1946, the airfield was put on Care and Maintenance.

Llanbedr, Gwynedd.

In 1940, a narrow coastal plain between the sand dunes of Morfa Dyffryn and the village of Llanbedr was requisitioned for the development of a forward fighter base. The airfield consisted of two concrete and tarmac runways, 05/23 4,328 feet and 16/34 4,207 feet, with one T2 and four Blister type hangars. It was officially opened as a RAF camp on 15 June 1941, under the control of RAF Valley. The first front line operational squadron to use Llanbedr for fighter cover was No. 74 Squadron, equipped with Supermarine Spitfires, from 4 October 1941 to 24 January 1942. Several other fighter squadrons and detachments were stationed at Llanbedr for most of the war, providing air and sea patrols in the vicinity. By the summer of 1942, enemy activity had diminished and the airfield reverted to its role as gunnery training base.

Pembrey, Carmarthenshire.

Pembrey airfield was officially opened on 6 May 1940, although the airfield had been in use since August 1939. The airfield is located on a site known as Towyn Burrows, some two miles from Burry Port. Originally,

Aerial photograph of Pembrey airfield.

the airfield was to have a grass landing area, but due to frequent flooding, three concrete and tarmac runways were built (5,200 feet, 4,020 feet and 3,540 feet) with twenty-seven dispersal pans. By the end of the war, four F Type, two Cranwell, and thirteen Blister type hangars had been constructed. On 20 June 1940, the airfield was transferred to No. 10 Group Fighter Command to provide air defence in the south Wales area and convoy protection.

The first fighter unit to be based at Pembrey was No. 92 Squadron, equipped with Spitfires, on 18 June 1940. Due to considerable enemy night activity in the area, night fighter units were stationed at the airfield in January 1941.

With the building of airfields at Fairwood and Angle, the importance of Pembrey as a fighter station diminished; in June 1941 Pembrey was transferred to Flying Training Command, but reverted back to Fighter Command in June 1945.

Aerial photograph of Pembroke Dock, the only flying boat station in Wales. (*B. Owen*)

Pembroke Dock, Pembrokeshire.

Pembroke Dock was the only flying boat station in Wales, and became one of the premier bases in the UK in this class.

The base was located on the south bank, opposite Neyland, and within the boundary of the town of Pembroke Dock. The main alighting area was Pembroke Reach, with a run of nearly 5,000 feet. The base was opened on 1 January 1930, but the first unit to be based at the flying station was No. 210 Squadron in June 1931. Throughout the 1930s, several flying boat units were based at Pembroke Dock and it was during this time that the base was gradually modified and the facilities expanded. Two large modified B Type and one T hangar were constructed as well as an elegant Georgian style Officers' mess. At least eleven Sunderland operational squadrons were based at Pembroke Dock between 1939 and 1945, covering a patrol area of the Bay of Biscay, the Western Approaches, and well into the Atlantic Ocean. RAF Pembroke Dock was officially closed on 31 March 1957.

Penrhos, Gwynedd.

The RAF camp at Penrhos was opened on 1 February 1937 as No. 5 Armament Training Station, using the nearby range at Hells Mouth. It was situated three miles west of Pwllheli, on the Llyn Peninsula, just off the A499 Abersoch road. The airfield, a circular grass area bounded by a concrete perimeter track, was built on a low plateau with the landing area south-west bound, some ten feet above the surrounding fields. Nine Bellman, one F Type, and the Extra Over Blister hangars were situated at the northern end, together with technical and domestic buildings.

Although not classed as a fighter or a bombing station, training aircraft at Penrhos were often involved in local patrols. Following enemy bombing of the airfield and surrounding area, detachments of fighters were eventually based at Penrhos. This continued more or less until Llanbedr and Valley became operational. RAF Penrhos finally closed on 31 March 1946.

St David's, Pembrokeshire.

The airfield was situated just off the A487 Haverfordwest to St David's road, 3½ miles from Brawdy. St David's airfield had three 150 feet-wide tarmac runways, measuring 5,910 feet, 3,200 feet and 3,570 feet in length. Along the perimeter track, there were thirty diamond/spectacle shaped hard standings in clusters of five. On the southern end there were three T2 hangars, associated workshops, headquarters, an administration office, and accommodation huts. St David's airfield was opened in September 1943 under No. 19 Group Coastal Command as a chain of the command's coastal airfields. The first unit to arrive at the airfield was No. 517 Squadron, equipped with Handley Page Halifaxes, on 26 November 1943. Another two Halifax units, Nos 502 and 517, joined in December. The squadrons were involved in anti-submarine and convoy patrols. On 2 February 1944, No. 517 Squadron moved to RAF Brawdy.

Due to the alignment of the runways with the prevailing winds, the Halifaxes could not take off fully loaded; they had to take off on a light load and proceed to Brawdy to top up and arm. It was a big drawback during operations, and, as a result, Brawdy became the main Headquarters base, and St David's was reverted to a satellite. For a brief time in 1945, Nos 53 and 220 Squadrons, equipped with Liberators, were based at St David's. On 1 November 1945, the airfield was put on Care and Maintenance and was eventually handed over to the Admiralty on 1 January 1946.

Talbenny, Pembrokeshire.

RAF Talbenny is situated on an escarpment overlooking St Bride's Bay, some three miles from Dale airfield. It had three concrete and tarmac

Aerial photograph of Talbenny from a circling aircraft.

A Vickers Wellington TX of No. 304 Squadron over the Pembrokeshire coast. (*via Polish War Archives*)

runways of 4,800 feet, 3,300 feet and 3,000 feet, with some thirty-six 'frying pan' type hard standings, sufficient for the parking of two fully equipped squadrons.

The airfield officially came to existence on 1 May 1942, under No. 19 Group, RAF Coastal Command, with Dale to the south as its satellite station. The first squadron to be stationed at Talbenny was No. 311, a Czech manned bomber squadron equipped with Vickers Wellington ICs. Both No. 311 and its sister unit No. 304, based at Dale, were involved in anti-submarine patrols and enemy shipping strikes in the Bay of Biscay and the Western Approaches. To provide fighter cover for the Wellingtons, detachments of Beaufighters from Nos 235 and 248 Squadrons were also based at Talbenny in January/February 1943.

Shipping strikes came to an end in May 1943 and No. 311 Squadron left Talbenny and returned to Bomber Command. Coastal Command Ferry Training Units became residents at the Airfield. Talbenny was taken over by Transport Command and used as a weather diversionary airfield. The airfield was finally closed on 23 December 1946.

Aerial photograph of RAF Valley in 1943. (*Welsh Assembly Archives*)

Valley, Anglesey.

RAF Valley is situated off the A5 road, close to the village of Caergeiliog and a mile from the village of Valley. The airfield was built to provide fighter cover for shipping, and to protect the industrial areas, ports and military bases of the north-west and Irish Sea.

The airfield had three concrete and tarmac runways of 4,800 feet, 4,200 feet and 3,900 feet, which were extended several times during the war. Initially, the airfield had two Type T2s, three Bellman, and four Blister hangars.

The airfield was opened on 1 February 1941 as a Fighter Sector Station under the control of No. 9 Group Fighter Command. The first fighter unit to be based at Valley was a detachment of Hurricane Mk Is of No. 312 (Czech) Squadron from Speke, Liverpool. To cope with the enemy night bombing raids, 'A' Flight of No. 219 Squadron, equipped with Bristol Beaufighter IFs, arrived at Valley. Over the next few years, other night fighter units were based at the airfield.

Squadrons based at Valley provided air defence cover for the area, especially in the Irish Sea and the north Wales coast. Numerous convoy escorts were flown by fighters from Valley, and later in the war the squadrons provided escort for United Sates aircraft entering and leaving Britain. On 19 June 1943, the USAAF Ferry Terminal became operational and from then on the airfield concentrated on American aircraft movements.

The RAF Fighter Sector closed on 1 November 1943, but two squadrons remained for night fighting and escort duties. By the end of 1943, all fighter units had left Valley. Today, Valley is the only active RAF station left in Wales.

Wrexham, Denbighshire (Clwyd).

RAF Wrexham was built south of the village of Borras, just off the A534 road and about three miles north-east of Wrexham town centre. The airfield was opened on 17 July 1941, under the control of No. 9 Group, as a fighter base for night fighters. The airfield consisted of three concrete runways measuring 4,680 feet, 4,050 feet and 3,300 feet. There were several fighter dispersal points: one Bellman, three Super Robin and four blister hangars. The main camp was on the west side of the airfields. No. 96 (night fighter) Squadron was based at the airfield from 21 October 1941 to 20 October 1942. Afterwards, RAF Wrexham reverted to training until it closed in September 1945.

The other airfields on Welsh soil were involved in training and providing target towing facilities to RAF fighters, army gunners, and warships. Maintenance Units were built for storage and aircraft modifications. The rest of the airfields were classed as Relief Landing Grounds, Storage Landing Grounds, and Emergency Landing Areas. Every base was an important factor in very well-oiled military machine, designed to keep the sea lanes open and the skies free of enemy bombers.

Acknowledgements

The author would like to extend special thanks to the following for their contributions:

Airfields Research Group
Air Heritage (Wales)
Australian Archives
CADW
Caernarfon Aero Park
Canadian Archives
Deric Brock
Gerry Evans
John Evans
Fleet Air Arm Museum, Yeovilton
Martin Hale
Imperial War Museum
Lloyds Shipping Records
Military Airfields of Wales (Bridge Books)
National Museum of Wales
No. 304 (Polish) Squadron Archives
David Ellis-Jones – Airship photographs and information
Ben Owen
Pembrokeshire Aviation Group
Morgan Parry
Public Records Offices (various)
Public Libraries – Pembrokeshire (various)
                 – Gwynedd (various)
                 – Swansea.
RAF Museum, Cosford
RAF Museum, Hendon

Mrs Ida Rowlands
South Wales Evening Post
Subterranean Britannica
Welsh Assembly Government (Photographic Archives)
Western Mail
Western Telegraph
Valley Aviation Society

Also, I would like to thank numerous individuals who contributed a wealth
of information towards the book; without their assistance and up to date
information, the book would not have been possible. Finally, my thanks
are extended to all who contributed photographs and illustrations.